Creating a Powerful Brand

IT'S NOT JUST BUSINESS, IT'S PERSONAL

Creating a Powerful Brand

IT'S NOT JUST BUSINESS, IT'S PERSONAL

ANDREW FORD

Dedicated to my two beautiful sons,
who challenge and reward me daily.

CONTENTS

Foreword

Marketers love brands. Just like the original cattle farmers who proudly marked their herd with their branding irons, marketers set out to create something that people see as different, relevant, and of a quality and reputation that people talk about and are willing to pay more for.

Marketers also love insights. Human truths they can tap into. Truths that spark ideas and make consumers say, 'Yes, they're talking to me, I'll try that.' Here's four that have stood the test of time: people like to tell others about great experiences they've had; people want their fifteen minutes of fame; businesspeople like to network and stay connected; and people want to know more about interesting celebrities, politicians, businesspeople, work colleagues and friends. These four age-old insights spawned brands such as Facebook, Instagram, YouTube, LinkedIn, Twitter and blogs.

Social media took the world by storm in the mid-2000s, and the marketing world not long after. While the early adopters of social media told their friends about their every move, marketers began to tap into the social footprint they were leaving. It was a win-win situation. People wanted to share their experiences with their friends as quickly as they could. Marketers wanted to be able to tap into those people's experiences so they could better understand them, and therefore create more relevant and personalised offers.

In leaving their social footprint, people were also inadvertently or deliberately creating a very public digital persona of themselves. Their likes and dislikes; their values and behaviours; their quirks and differences; their reputation. People were creating their own brand.

Marketers had dabbled with the thought of people as brands back in the late 1990s. In fact, a study back then saw Ian Thorpe appear as one of Australia's top brands. It was the inevitable evolution of agents, managers and PR practitioners crafting the reputations of many a sports star, actor or musician into marketable commodities. But now marketers wanted to know how their brand fitted with the personal brand of their endorser. Understanding how to create and maintain a personal brand became very important indeed.

Fast forward to 2013, and many are beginning to realise the importance of their digital and social footprint, and in turn their reputation and their personal brand. In writing this book, Andrew Ford empowers you to create and maintain the personal brand that is you.

Andrew Baxter
CEO, Ogilvy Australia
Twitter: @andrewbaxter3
LinkedIn: au.linkedin.com/in/andrewbaxter3/

Introduction

'Seek and you shall understand.'
Tao philosophy

In my favourite movie, *The Matrix*, machines have taken over the world and are using humans as batteries. In the film, the character Morpheus says a brilliant line to the newly awakened Neo: 'Welcome to the real world.'

Luckily, you and I aren't in *The Matrix*, but there are still parallels in the modern world as computers have, in many ways, taken over our lives. People don't leave the house without their smart phone, social media is always being checked, the internet can answer all of our questions instantly and we expect constant connectivity. Mobiles, tablets and laptops are ever present in even the remotest communities and the world has shrunk to fit into the palm of our hands. Many Gen Y people I know don't own watches, alarm clocks or cameras as they have these on one device in their pockets at all times. While the role of computers in our lives is less obtrusive than it is in *The Matrix*, it still underpins our daily behaviour.

In recent decades, technology has completely changed how the world works, especially in relation to business. How people interact, their perspective of time, how they consume media and advertising and how they purchase products is vastly different than it was even ten years ago. But how can small business owners and entrepreneurs use this trend to their advantage?

In our new business world, traditional media, such as television, newspapers, radio and billboards – which I call 'push' marketing – aren't as effective as they once were. These mediums were once used to inform and convince consumers about what brands to buy and from where, and for the last 100 years they have been central to marketing. Today, social media like LinkedIn, Facebook and Twitter, and a host of free tools, such as Google, DropBox, 99 Designs, Squarespace, GoDaddy, WordPress, Klout, Hoot Suite and many more, have made new forms of marketing both cheap and efficient for businesses. Now when a business wants to sell its products, it can build a simple website for a very low cost, be found on Google and social media and easily reach its desired consumers. This is significantly disrupting many industries, as consumers are empowered with advanced search features on their phones, tablets and laptops so they can talk directly to businesses without the need for channels such as wholesalers, retailers and traditional advertising companies.

Think of the once-ubiquitous *Yellow Pages* business directory, a huge book delivered to your door once a year. I worked for Australia's *Yellow Pages*, marketing the competitive digital products, and I saw first hand the demise of a billion-dollar business in only five years, while digital grew exponentially. Luckily for me, I was the Digital Marketing Manager! I experienced the digital revolution changing the way small businesses went about attracting clients. It is a change in the way people think about advertising and worth exploring to ensure it is crystal clear.

THE DIGITAL REVOLUTION

The digital revolution has been rapid. First consumers used search engines to find businesses and products they wanted, prompting the website revolution. Then consumers started asking their friends on social media such as Facebook for advice; today they search in applications on their phones for trusted sources such as review sites and peer opinions. They seek out brands that resonate with them, run by people they feel they can trust and relate to. Owners who have a cause and passion for what they do, who are not just a business seeking profit. The change in the market has been significant, and it's only just begun.

This change has prompted the rise of the authentic entrepreneur, someone who genuinely cares about his or her products and customers. No longer can this be faked, hence the popular use of the word 'authenticity'. Companies that are dishonest are quickly found out and ostracised. Just google 'Cadbury palm oil' for an example of a company having to change their ways due to public pressure[6]. Some of this change has been driven by inspirational companies such as Apple Inc., which aspired to excellence in everything they did due to their authentic and visionary leader, Steve Jobs. Compare Apple Inc. to their competitors and you will find organisations whose vision is to make financial goals, not improve the world. I worked for both IBM and Hewlett-Packard during the rise of Apple Inc. and saw both sides. This is one of the major changes in the consumer psyche: *the quest to find meaning in their consumption.* Those that can fulfil this need will be successful, and those that don't will merely survive. The key to this is running a Personal Business, which is underpinned by a leader with an authentic and powerful Personal Brand. This book aims to provide you the mindset of the new marketing era, as well as an overview of the tools required to harness the new technology.

Let us begin, now.

Andrew Ford
'The Brand Man'
2 November 2013

---

[6] www.news.com.au/business/cadbury-removes-palm-oil/story-e6frfm1i-1225764168405, 2 November 2013

CHAPTER 1

Marketing in the Digital Age

'New marketing is about the relationships, not the medium.'
Ben Grossman

How did this book find its way into your hands? Was it a gift, did someone tell you about it, did you search for it online or did you come across my social media and then follow the links to my website? Perhaps you bought it at one of my training courses, or you are one of my consulting clients. However it fell into your hands, it is unlikely you were browsing in a bookshop and just happened to come across it. You probably didn't see an advertisement in the newspaper or receive a leaflet in your letterbox either. Most probably you would have heard about the book through word of mouth via a digital medium like Google, Twitter, Facebook or LinkedIn.

Think about it for a moment: only a matter of years ago you would have *only* been able to buy this book in a bookshop. Today, that is the *last* place you would have found it. This simple example demonstrates the massive change in consumer shopping behaviour aided by technology. It doesn't mean there are no more bookshops left or that traditional methods of reaching consumers are dead; far from it. What it means is that there are now *alternatives* that can be extremely useful, cost-effective and beneficial to your business. The importance of these changes depends on what type of industry your business is in.

Some industries have been significantly disrupted, creating tremendous opportunities for businesses and entrepreneurs. Think music, books, advertising, recruitment and retail. In these industries the multiple barriers between buyers and sellers have been removed. Consumers can now find information and transact without the aid of the many layers of marketing, media, large companies and human intervention. It is the era of the consumer-to-consumer marketing, and to take advantage of these changes and aid your creation of a Personal Business plan, you need to understand a little more about advertising.

THE ADVERTISING REVOLUTION

After working in marketing for fifteen years in some of the world's largest companies, plus consulting to high-profile athletes, models, actors and business professionals, I realised that the traditional approach to promotion and advertising was not as effective as it once was. I saw that there were new ways of getting messages to target customers faster, cheaper and more efficiently.

Imagine if, instead of bombarding everyone with your message in the hope of hitting a customer who wanted your product, your customers found you! Luckily, the technology enabling this dream to be a reality is now available. This technology is very effective, virtually free, and readily available to all; however, you need to know a few rules to leverage it. We will explore this soon, but first, it's worthwhile reflecting on why these changes have occurred.

Traditional advertising includes television, radio, newspapers, magazines and billboards, plus other means of reaching customers such as the *Yellow Pages*, catalogues and cold calling. But now there are so many variations of these traditional media channels that it can be confusing to non-marketing people. For instance, television used to purely consist of free-to-air commercial stations that provided entertainment to the consumer in exchange for the opportunity to show advertising. The model – or value exchange – was that if you wanted to watch TV for free, you had to put up with the ads.

Then people began creating technology that enabled consumers to skip advertising. TV stations reacted by putting more ads in commercial breaks, product placement into shows, visual ads into sports and a myriad other ways of reaching viewers. However, consumers don't like ads because only a few will be meaningful to them, so they paid even less attention. Advertising companies – eager to make ever-increasing revenue – responded with yet more advertising. The more they pushed, the more consumers retreated. This cycle has played out in every advertising sector, be it television, radio or billboards. It seems you can't leave your house without being besieged by advertising messages. Notice how many you see next time you are going to work. It's scary when you do.

Advertisers were forced to become more creative and put more advertising into content to trick consumers into watching them. Think of all the product placements in TV and movies, celebrity endorsements, infomercials based around advertising and reality TV. They even made ads even more annoying so that they stood out! The result was that consumers became so inundated by messages that they just didn't notice them as much, and their level of trust in the message was massively reduced.

Frustrated consumers decided to get their information from more trusted sources, such as their friends and other consumers. Think of all the sites that rely on consumer reviews, such as eBay, Facebook business pages and restaurant and travel review sites. Even LinkedIn is a review site for people with the advent of recommendations and endorsements. Now the advertisers were out of the loop completely – they had bastardised their channel of communication so much that consumers had shut them out.

Consumers created new ways of deciding which brands, companies and products suited their needs and were cool. For the first time in a hundred years, the advertising model of business to consumer (B2C) had become the age of consumer to consumer (C2C). Consumers now had the power to make or break brands, and what they thought about the brand became reality. Corporate and media control of consumers was reduced, not completely, but much more than in previous generations.

In this new era, companies must listen to their customers and encourage them to tell their friends to recommend their brand! Consumer power is here and you can take advantage of that for your business. It is an incredible opportunity. Follow the principles in this book, understand technology and yourself, build your Personal Brand in social media and leverage your Personal Business to attract new and exciting opportunities.

MARKETING IS INFORMATION

The evolution of the smart phone, wi-fi (invented in Australia by the CSIRO, by the way), search engines and social media have revolutionised not only advertising, but basic human communication too. People can share information instantly and regularly, they feel more empowered to make their own choices and they don't need to be 'told' what to buy – they will make up their own minds. When consumers consider a product, they talk about it to their friends, experts in the field and even complete strangers, and trust their advice over that of the business selling the product.

For marketing to be successful, it now needs to shift from telling people what to do, to *informing* them. Instead of selling a dream, your message should be authentic, transparent and genuine. No longer can you promote the advantages of your product and ignore the downsides, as previous users of it will have already shared the good, the bad and the ugly somewhere online. Review sites are everywhere, and there is instant access to information about every company, brand and product, so you can't hide.

These are the three rules of the new online marketing world: authenticity, transparency and individuality. If you provide anything less, your community will lose faith in you. Gone is the age of spreading a message to a captive audience through one-way communication channels. There are now communities of consumers who can be engaged through two-way relationships. This point is really important.

There has been a fundamental change in consumer behaviour over the past few years. A statistic from a 2013 Neilsen report states that eighty per cent of consumers trust peer recommendations, which is the highest form of trust in communications.[7] This is not just a small change in consumer sentiment, but a massive cultural phenomenon that has transformed the marketing and advertising industries in a significant and permanent way. People have always trusted their friends, but now the ability to communicate these opinions has massively increased due to technology.

In this new landscape, I believe that branding is the key to business success. Things such as your logo and your company name form only a small part of your brand. Central to a successful

---

[7] http://www.nielsen.com/us/en/newswire/2013/under-the-influence-consumer-trust-in-advertising.html

brand is what consumers think of you; essentially, it's your reputation. This is developed in every interaction you have with customers, from how you answer the phone to how you advertise, to the look and feel of your website. All your interactions with clients affect your brand. You need to focus on branding yourself or a product/service in a personal way, usually in order for your target market to get to know, like and trust you, or in order to build a relationship with them, rather than simply marketing impersonal business opportunities/products/services to them.

In the past, companies could control the messages related to their brands via exclusive and trusted advertising channels. As discussed, this is no longer the case, and consumers have the power to make or break brands based on discussions online. Do you know what consumers are saying about your brand? If not, you'd better find out!

So if consumers are the new advertising channel, how do you take advantage of this new medium? The answer is to build a business around the people.

CHAPTER 2

Your Personal Business

'Strive not to be a success,
but rather to be of value.'
Albert Einstein

A Personal Business means that you are your business. It's not enough to simply be running an enterprise: you need to be *visibly* running it. A Personal Business is one where the products and services are devised by the founders, mostly to solve a problem they have experienced, and often because they experienced a void relating to it in the past. They feel compelled to solve a problem and are fiercely determined to do so. The marketing is driven mainly by their personalities, using social media and networking as well as the traditional methods. These people are authentic and transparent and their customers buy from them as much because of their story as the utility of the goods. These authentic entrepreneurs use their Personal Brands as one of the driving forces in their marketing and because of this, their customers search for and find them. They can reach around the world in an instant, so can be in tiny niche industries yet thrive in the world marketplace, not just their local one. There are hundreds of examples of these digital entrepreneurs; just think of the products and services you buy each day. I am one of them, perhaps you are too. Your Facebook is probably full of your friends promoting a cause or business they are passionate about – this is how Richard Branson of Virgin fame operated his business and he didn't possess any of the amazing tools we have at our disposal today.

The cultural shift of consumers is the underlying force and this is driven by our need for meaning in our lives. According the Maslow's hierarchy of needs, once we have satisfied our basic safety and survival requirements we seek meaning or self-actualisation. The past couple of generations haven't encountered a lack of consumer goods – it's actually the opposite – so their psyche now searches not just for satisfaction from purchases, but for meaning. This is why people love to tell you that their coffee is fair trade from villagers in Columbia and their tablet is made by Apple Inc. They want their purchases to *mean* something, not just *do* something. Satisfy this requirement and your customers will love your brand, not just like it.

How do we create meaningful brands, I hear you ask? The answer is that there are no short cuts; it takes time and effort, and cannot be faked or bought. The good news is that you have everything you need right now, inside of you, because the answer is *you*. You are the driving force behind your company and brand. Therefore, if you discover your passion, your drivers, your story, you just need to build a platform to tell it and your perfect consumers will seek you out.

By following the principles in this book I am certain that you can build your Personal Business platform around your very own Personal Brand. It doesn't matter if you are working for another company or your own; the principles apply equally well to both. Technology and cultural changes affect small business owners and entrepreneurs the same as they affect individuals managing their own careers. Gone are the days of working for one company for your whole career. Job security is a thing of the past so it is up to each individual to run their career as their own Personal Business. Therefore, taking advantage of digital tools to manage your Personal Brand is just as useful for an individual as it is for a small business owner or entrepreneur. LinkedIn now rules job search so it is worthwhile to have the best profile possible, as most companies will search your digital profile before hiring you. (They will also review your other social media so protect yourself, as a lot of people *don't* get hired due to what they put online.)

So, just about everyone can now take advantage of the Personal Business revolution, whether you are working for others or starting your own business. Throughout this book, I will show you simple strategies and tools that are available to anyone with a laptop, smartphone, internet access and imagination.

You don't need a high level of marketing or technology knowledge to read this – in fact, it's the opposite. I have aimed this book at supporting those who could not even spell the word 'internet', to teach them the basics of technology, marketing and social media, all the way to constructing their own personal brands and digital marketing campaigns. Sounds like a challenge? Believe me, it is possible!

I have taken many clients who are in your situation today from being fearful and confused to confident and empowered. Everyone begins their journey with differing levels of experience in this subject, and some have a fear of technology or a lack of self-belief in their ability to get 'it'. Some don't know where to start, some know what to do but need a third-party opinion, others love the coaching aspect of my services. The fact you are reading this tells me you know what I am talking about, that you share some of these needs. Because everyone is at a different level, I have written the material with the most inexperienced reader in mind. For some of you some of the chapters will be very basic and will require only a brief read; for others, each chapter will provide significant learnings.

Even though I have had over twenty years work experience and several degrees in the marketing field, I am not professing to be the master of everything digital. Rather, I have specific experiences and an approach to helping clients that many people have found useful, and it is my goal to be able to impart some of this knowledge on you, to help in your business. I hope this knowledge helps you in understanding another way to approach marketing in your business.

The first concept is called 'Three Paths', and it relates to how customers find you.

THE THREE PATHS

There are only three paths consumers will follow to find your business: people, brands or products.

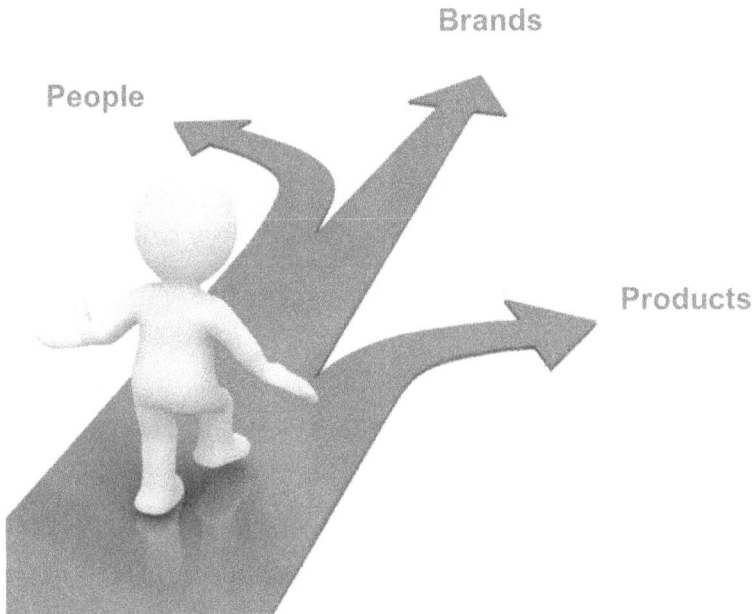

The traditional way consumers found businesses was through brands. Companies would open a shop, and advertise in print publications, TV, radio and other traditional media so that their brand names were remembered. Consumers would see these messages, remember the brands and then when a need arose they would seek out these brands to purchase. A great example of this advertising was IBM. Consumers trusted the brand via reputation and advertising; even though you couldn't buy an IBM, you bought their products. However, most of their advertising focused on promoting their name, so when you wanted a product they sold, you would know and trust the products with an IBM badge.

Once the internet arrived and consumers had the ability to search for what they desired themselves, company brands became less important and the products, or more specifically the product utility, became another way of finding companies. Utility is a marketing term to define the value the product or service provides the consumer. In this mode consumers wouldn't search for company brands like IBM, but on their need; for example, a cheap laptop or gaming laptop. They would then be presented with all the product options from various companies, including IBM.

The next phase was consumers searching on specific people, not the company or product, using search engines and also social media. For instance, using our laptop example, consumers can use Google to look up a laptop review site, go on a LinkedIn user group, ask questions on their Facebook news feed or search for 'gaming' experts and ask their advice on which laptop to buy. In this scenario, the consumer isn't relying on company-provided information or advertising, they are using other consumers to gather their information.

Consumers use all three mechanisms to find the right product, so it is important to have a strategy for all three. Most companies I have worked with already have advertising and digital strategies for their brands and products, but have overlooked the people element.

The people marketing strategy is what makes a Personal Business personal. It's about the people inside the business, the leaders, the experts, but also the people connected to the business such as partners, as well as customers. All of these people can either help or hinder your business so it is important to have a strategy for all areas.

There are many ways to build an effective people marketing strategy, depending on the type of business you are in. I consult with individuals who want a great LinkedIn presence for the right career opportunities, small business owners who want to attract more customers, and larger corporations that want to protect their company reputations and use their staff more effectively. Regardless of the situation, the foundation principles are the same. It all begins with Personal Branding. Having a great online presence for you and your staff is paramount in setting up a Personal Business. Then leveraging your staff or yourself with your partners and customers is the next step in the process to attract more opportunities to your business.

To do this, we follow three key Personal Branding steps: understand, build and leverage.

Understand **Build** **Leverage**

'Understand' means getting to really know you and what your brand represents, your products or services, and your clients and what they really want.

'Build' means constructing your Personal Business and Personal Brand in digital media around these understandings.

'Leverage' means using these new digital tools to optimise and grow your brand for business benefit.

To start this process we need to understand ourselves, and this begins with the 'Why'.

THE WHY

A Personal Business and consequently an authentic Personal Brand is based on the 'Why?'. Why do you do what you do? Why did you choose that career? Why did you start that particular business? What drives you to work at solving this challenge for people? Why do you love serving these particular customers? If you are in a career you love, there will be a fundamental psychological answer to all of these questions. If you don't love your career or business, perhaps it's time to start looking for what you do love. Let's use me as an example to clarify the process.

I have always had an interest in psychology and what drives people. So of course I am interested in what drives *me*. I also loved business, hence the attraction to marketing, to blend these two interests. That is a logical answer; however, the more I thought about it and searched for my underlying motivation, the more I realised that what you do is fundamentally inter-linked with who you are. If you follow your passions and listen to your intuition, your business will represent who you are. You can't help constructing a career or business around your values and beliefs, hence your business is *Personal*. Your business is a reflection of you, and your Personal Brand is a reflection of your business. Your perfect clients are those who resonate with your business and brand because it matches their beliefs. Therefore, if you are not congruent with your beliefs or don't communicate them effectively, how can you attract your perfect client? Without control of your online brand you can't communicate your business or brand, and your clients can't find you or understand if they want to connect with you.

So back to my 'why'. Why did I spend all my holidays, weekends and weeknights after putting the kids to bed, writing this book? Why do I run a business helping people with their Personal Brands? Sometimes I think I am crazy, given that I have a full-time business, two young children, a significant exercise program, friendships and relationships to maintain; yet I am compelled to keep going. Perhaps I am crazy, but crazy people have a habit of doing incredible things. I believe I am living my life to the fullest, following where my intuition takes me.

To share my why, I need to delve into my personal life, which is a little confronting but it's important to share the process with my readers. It is the process I take my clients through and can get quite deep and personal, as that is the nature of the work. If you find this confronting you can skip to the next section if you'd prefer, but I hope that by explaining what drives me, it might help you understand your own journey. To create a Personal Business you must know what drives *you*. So with your permission, here goes.

My journey began early. In fact, it began on the day I was born. That was the day that my father decided to leave, never to be part of my life again. He left me with my mother and two young siblings, without money or support – a seemingly selfish and callous decision. That single event set a course for my life that would bring me to writing this book right now. What's the connection, you might wonder. Well, what neither my father nor I realised at the time was that he set me free. Free to be whatever I wanted in this world, free of the traditional model of a man, father, worker, or anything else. Even though my mum taught me valuable wisdom and life lessons, there was still a void. Of course grandparents and various role models came in to help fill the void, however, to a young boy a father is probably the single biggest influence on their lives and for me this was missing.

I didn't have an obvious example for what I 'should' be in many aspects of life, so I had to work it out by myself. I had to research, choose and create, rather than replicate – from teaching myself about the ways of girls, complexities of money and career choices, to simple things like how to ride a bike, to shave and fix things. I had to seek out information, assess the best decisions and trust my instincts. Everything I have and believe in has been my choice, instead of being passed down by a strong figure. When my dad left, he created a void for a mentor and teacher, so I search for these people in my life to this day. I had a choice: I could follow in his footsteps and be a recalcitrant dad drifting through life, or make something of myself. I chose the latter. In fact I still have vivid memories of the moments when as a young boy facing some challenging situations I had to 'man' up and make some decisions about who I wanted to be, how I would act and principles I wanted to live by.

This background explains my commitment to self-improvement. I have worked hard at gathering knowledge via formal education, searched out best-practice alternative thinking and challenged myself to be the man I wanted to be. I am passionate about teaching and mentoring others and being a proactive and connected dad. This is my why. It started from birth and continues to drive me to this day.

My upbringing was quite unusual for the times. I spent time in ashrams, experienced the Indian cult Orange People, went to church once a week, studied Buddhism, threw myself into martial arts, read science texts on metaphysics and attended many personal development camps and courses. These activities were mostly sponsored by my mother, who I cannot thank enough for such a diverse upbringing.

I loved business as I saw the love my grandparents had for theirs and the benefits it provided our family. So of course I wanted that for me. In fact, I never really thought much about my mission in life until my eldest son, Hudson, asked me what I had dreamt of doing when I was a kid his age, which was seven at the time. I thought for a while and realised that all I really wanted to do was work in business. His response was touching: 'Well Dad, you get to live your dream then.' And I guess he is right. Even better, I get to help others to live their dreams by discovering their why and crafting their own businesses.

I've devoted a great deal of time to formal education. I've been awarded a Bachelor Degree in Marketing, graduating with a Distinction, an Associate Diploma in Management after two years studying a Masters of Business Administration (Executive), and a Masters of Business in Entrepreneurship and Innovation. I've won business plan competitions at Swinburne University and business strategy contests for Boston Consulting Group, and I now judge entrepreneur pitch competitions on a regular basis for various groups such as Key Persons of Influence, Melbourne University and Startup Weekend. As I like to tell my clients, I studied for fifteen years at university so that they don't have to!

I also committed to developing my body, and trained in many of the martial arts disciplines, such as judo (in which I have a green belt), aikido, arnis (stick fighting) and karate, in which I gained a first-degree black belt and instructed for several years. I also became a Level 1 Canadian ski instructor and have completed many triathlons, and countless swimming, riding and running races, to balance mental and physical activity. I believe the mind and body work in harmony – so a strong body supports my mental activity. It also powers my ability to chase my kids up trees!

All of my experiences – work, education, sport, travel and family – have balanced my life and provided me with perspective to be able to teach. Once I had developed enough knowledge, work experience and perhaps more importantly, life experience, I had a tremendous desire to give back. After teaching karate for many years, teaching my kids on a daily basis and mentoring several junior work colleagues, I jumped at the opportunity to lecture at university when it arrived. For three years, I shared my knowledge of digital marketing and branding with Masters of Marketing students.

During my time lecturing, I was approached to share my experience more directly with colleagues and friends, so I began Social Star. I love to help people uncover their missions, learn their strengths and understand their personality so they can develop their Personal Businesses. It took me years to develop my own knowledge, processes and Personal Brand, and I now pass on what I've learnt to you. Everyone has a purpose; most people haven't discovered it yet or have forgotten what it feels like to really love what they do. My hope for you is that you find your passion and purpose, if you haven't already, and find the tools in this book useful to help you create the business you love to work in.

So enough about me: think about you. What is your why? If you look closely you can see it in your life – how the why drives your behaviour. What does your life demonstrate? You will see patterns in behaviour that will show you clearly what drives you. It is neither good nor bad, it just is. Understanding your why and how it influences your life can greatly assist you in finding a career and business that fits your need. If you have your own business, it drives your inspiration and flow. Your Personal Brand will reflect it and if you are transparent you will attract like-minded people to your life and attract opportunities. If they connect with you authentically it doesn't really matter what you sell; they will want to buy it. They feel it will be made with quality and purpose because they trust you. This is why a strong Personal Brand is so vital to your business.

CHAPTER 3

Personal Branding

'A brand is no longer what we tell the consumer it is – it is what consumers tell each other it is.'
Scott Cook

Everyone knows great brands. They advertise on TV, you wear them on your body, you buy them at the supermarket, you tell your friends about them and you might even queue up over-night to get their latest products! Apple, Nike, Coca Cola, Virgin and Google are great examples. We know them and we love them, but these brands do not come about organically – they are manufactured by marketing teams, branding experts and various media. In short, they are created, not born.

For many years, companies have created brands from prod-ucts and services with specific attributes – a certain look and feel – and then imbued them with a three-dimensional person-ality through marketing. This is the same process we will follow to create a Personal Brand for you. But first, let's define what a Personal Brand is.

Tom Peters first coined the term Personal Branding in his classic 1997 *Fast Company* article *The Brand Called You*[8], in which he describes it as an individual who markets their personal strengths, attributes, and qualities.

Another description by Blaise James, Gallup global brand strategist and former strategic planning director at Ogilvy & Mather Worldwide, is, "Your personal brand isn't a couple of adjectives, and it shouldn't be a résumé either. It should demonstrate your authentic talents and strengths. Your self-brand is integral to your career and your life – and it influences your long-term career strategy and development.[9]"

I love this description as it captures the essence of the difference between your résumé and your brand. I stress the importance that a Personal Brand needs to have integrity and authenticity in order to really touch the hearts of your target consumers. A Personal Brand is one that allows the audience to immediately resonate with the culture, values and attributes of the brand.

A well-honed Personal Brand is made up of a few essential elements. First and foremost are quality pictures and robust words that definitively show a potential customer the values and attributes of a person and their business. Humans have 40 000

---

8 www.fastcompany.com/magazine/10/brandyou
9 http://businessjournal.gallup.com/content/121796/value-personal-branding.aspx

years of facial-recognition technology built into their subconscious brains. The response to personal photos in the digital world is no different from the way it works in the physical world. The brain still makes an immediate analysis of a face to determine whether it likes or distrusts that person. It is instant, so the clearer the photograph of a person is, the quicker and more accurately a viewer can make a judgement.

This is important because Personal Branding is as much about attracting the right types of clients to you as it is about prospective clients learning more about your services. It is no use enticing people to investigate your services if they will never end up using you, or worse, will engage you on a job that makes your life miserable because they aren't compatible with the values of your business. A strong, clear Personal Brand can filter out these consumers so that the people who investigate your product or service are more likely to purchase it and be satisfied.

The words you use online to articulate your brand are the second thing that potential clients will review, so it is equally important to have a professional assist you. Our conscious, logical mind needs to be convinced of the value a product or service provides. Quality words will help persuade the consumer to choose yours over others.

We will review how to create a Personal Brand in depth in the latter part of the book. But now, let's explore some of the rules for Personal Branding – namely, being authentic, transparent and individual.

HAVING AN AUTHENTIC BRAND

The number-one rule in modern marketing is to be authentic. The brand you are and the brand you want to be have to be aligned with your personal values and reflect your traits.

A great example of an authentic brand is Steve Jobs of Apple Inc. fame. Steve Jobs started Apple Inc. with his friends Steve Wozniak and Ronald Wayne back in 1976. Steve represented an image of himself to his staff and customers as a revolutionary inventor, one of the 'crazy people' like Einstein and Richard Branson. The authentic nature of Apple Inc. is related to their products, which are specifically produced in certain ways, no excuses. If you don't like them, don't buy them. You can find all of the information clearly on their website and they don't try to 'sell' you the products; they inform you about what they do. The products speak for themselves. They are for certain people, not for everyone, which is what being authentic to your passion is all about.

The authenticity of the business comes from its leaders and Mr Jobs was nothing if not clear about his intentions. My favourite quote is from the early days when he was trying to hire a new CEO. Remember, back then the company was tiny and just recovering from near bankruptcy. His strategy to poach the Pepsi-Cola CEO in 1983 was magnificent; Jobs said to John Sculley, 'Do you want to sell sugar water for the rest of your life, or do you want to come with me and change the world?' How is that for clarity!

TRANSPARENCY

Scott Cook's quote at the start of this chapter is brilliant in its simplicity, as it succinctly explains the changes that have occurred in marketing and branding – the power of your brand is no longer in your hands; it is in the hands of the consumer.

Online forums, review sites, price comparison sites and comment threads on Facebook provide consumers with broad knowledge about the marketplace. This is what economists mean by pure competition – a market where the prices and products of sellers are easily compared and consumers are fully informed. Consequently, prices are set by consumers, which means that a business with similar products to those of a competitor cannot set its prices higher. Today, we see this in many sectors of our economy, where traditional retailers struggle to maintain a foothold in the digital world due to so many 'e-tailers' offering the same products at lower prices.

The ease of information exchange online – accelerated by the boom in smartphone usage – has been central to this shift. So how does someone differentiate their products from those of their competitors when a consumer can compare prices on their mobile while standing in front of a salesperson? They must do it through a strong and clear brand that matches the values of consumers!

Be honest. Make a product you are proud of, that serves a genuine need for a group of consumers, do a great job and sell it for a fair price. This goes against modern marketing practices, but is the essence of what marketing actually is. Don't try to fake it as consumers will find out and your brand will be tarnished by that reputation. If you make a mistake, own up to it and be transparent about it.

A great example of transparency is Oprah Winfrey, one of the most successful women in the world. Her history is nothing short of astounding: 'Winfrey is best known for her multi-award-winning talk show *The Oprah Winfrey Show*, which was the highest-rated program of its kind in history and was nationally syndicated from 1986 to 2011. She has been ranked the richest African-American of the 20th century, the greatest black philanthropist in American history, and is currently North America's only black billionaire. She is also, according to some assessments, the most influential woman in the world.' (Quoted from Wikipedia, which is not an exact reference source, but it is what the general public uses, which is why I have used it here.) For someone who grew up in poverty, was a victim of teen rape and had an illegitimate child, to prosper so greatly is astonishing.

The reason we know so much about Oprah is that she is painfully transparent. People feel like they know her because she shares her story and faces her challenges with her audience. Basically she is real and inspirational. An honest person.

The amount you choose to share with your clients via your Personal Business really depends on the type of business you're in and your personality. That's why we do some much work in the Understand step of developing your brand, so you know how much of you to put into your brand and business. I usually ask my clients a very simple question: on a scale of 1 to 10, with 1 being Oprah and 10 being a brick, what level do you want to share your personality with your community? Then we construct the level of personalisation around this number.

INDIVIDUALITY

Be yourself. That is the key to finding out what you want to do in life; listen to your intuition and heart as they have all the information you need. Whether it is finding the job you love or building a company from scratch, if you base it upon your values and vision, it will fulfil you. Fulfilment doesn't necessarily equate to millions of dollars of profit – I am talking about a career you enjoy doing each day, in which you are proud of putting your name to your brand, and where external incentives are not required as you are inspired to serve the customers.

Finding this path is not easy, especially if you have invested significant time in developing a successful career based on a role where you like the perks but don't love the work. I understand, I have been there too and let me assure you that once you are in a career you truly love, the perks you thought were important quickly fade into insignificance against knowing that you are making a difference in the world.

Basing your career around your values and beliefs is the essence of a Personal Business, and if you do this you can't help but have an individual and very specific Personal Brand. Your brand is you, and it will resonate with the customers you love to serve and partners you want to spend time with. The more specific you are about what you want and who you are, the more you are able to attract the exact match to your desires. It is the same with dating – I have actually been asked to help with finding the perfect partner as the theory and methods are the same!

A great example of an individual brand is Warren Buffett, the world's most famous and successful investor. Haven't heard of him? If you read the financial press, such as Forbes, you will see his company Berkshire Hathaway is one of the largest companies in the world, and if you have ever purchased stocks from the stock market you would be shocked to know that the price of only one class A share in this company is worth over US$150,000. Yes, for only one share. You see, most companies split shares to keep the price low, but Warren Buffett decided he didn't want to do this. He also doesn't pay dividends, ever. Only once in the last fifty years has the company paid a dividend. Mr Buffett goes his own way, and because he listens to his own judgement rather those around him, he has been fantastically successful. In fact, he's more than twice as successful as the S&P 500 index over the past twenty years; not a bad average.

The examples above highlighting authenticity, transparency and individuality show that these traits are natural parts of those leaders' personalities. We all have these traits within us, focusing our efforts to produce a career where we can express these traits is the key to our success.

ADVANTAGES OF PERSONAL BRANDING

Before we rush off to create our Personal Businesses, let's look at the advantages and disadvantages of this process. I believe that all things have two sides, and it would be remiss of me not to explore these so you can choose how much you want to invest in the process based on your own unique values.

First, let's explore the advantages.

Imagine for a moment that you are a twelve-year-old boy in Canada who likes to sing and has a dream of being a super-star. How would you kick-start your dream? Ten years ago your choices were to send demo tapes to recording companies and enter talent contests. Today, you can use the power of social media to test your brand on an audience and see how many people resonate with what you have to offer. This is the ultimate product trial and the feedback you receive will show you where your audience is, and how engaged they are.

In 2007, an unknown twelve-year-old boy named Justin Bieber uploaded videos of himself singing on YouTube, among thousands of other aspiring musicians. He was discovered by talent manager Scooter Braun in 2008. Scooter saw potential in the young singer and introduced him to Usher, one of the biggest stars in American R&B. Interestingly, Usher didn't like Justin to start with, however, Justin believed in his dream and remained authentic to his brand and eventually won Usher over.

Justin is now the global pop star he dreamed of being, and has one of the most watched and commented on YouTube videos of all time in *Baby*, with almost 900 million views, nearly two million likes and more than three million dislikes! He isn't for everyone, but for those who match his values and personality, he is a direct hit. Justin put his unique self out there authentically and due to his talent, determination and uniqueness, he was picked up by the mainstream. First and foremost, however, his success sprang from his social media savvy.

Social media can launch careers and be an exciting marketing tool if the medium is understood and respected. Justin Bieber and Lady Gaga are great examples of how unknown musicians can become household names by leveraging social media. But it is not just celebrities who can use it. President Obama's campaign team has successfully used Twitter and Facebook during two elections to help him gain office[10].

DOWNSIDES OF PERSONAL BRANDING

I decided to include a picture of the Yin and Yang symbol at the start of this book as it is a powerful emblem to me – so much so that I have it tattooed on my wrist to remind me of balance in life. That there is no dark without light, no true joy without the experience of sadness, no appreciation for wealth without knowledge of being poor, no love without hate. Likewise,

---

[10] www.readwriteweb.com/archives/social_media_obama_mccain_comparison.php

successfully using Personal Branding will create many amazing opportunities, but it will also bring with it various challenges. In fact, you will encounter just as many challenges as you do today, but in a different form. However, this shouldn't stop you transforming your business into a Personal Business, as the downside of staying where you are could be going out of business altogether!

There are three possible pitfalls to consider when creating a Personal Brand. First, a robust Personal Brand will not make up for outdated products, ridiculously high prices or poor customer service. The relative power of your brand may attract people to buy your services, however, if you fail to deliver on a regular basis people will eventually discover that your brand is hollow and you will lose both your business and your credibility. Once you venture online you're inviting a double-edged sword of positive and negative information about your brand. You have probably seen this happen to celebrities endorsing random products without due diligence. Think of Australian cricketer Shane Warne, who was sponsored by nicotine-substitute company Nicorette and then got caught smoking; or Britney Spears, who was in an ad for Pepsi and was then photographed drinking Coke.

Before you create your Personal Brand, you may have to change your products and services to ensure that they match your values and ethos. Can you put your hand on your heart and fully stand behind every one of your products? Do you 100 per cent believe that they add significant value to people's lives? If not, change them. This is where the main challenge might be for your business. However, if you can delight your customers rather than just satisfying them, you will realise that this is when your job becomes a fulfilling mission and a life's work.

Second, the impact of becoming a high-profile person in an industry can have a significant effect on your personal life, so it is best to be prepared. It can be daunting to have photos and videos of yourself published online, and words written about you on websites, for all the world to see. The level of mental adjustment required to cope with this depends on how an individual values privacy and how closely their brand aligns to them. Once my clients understand that their online brand isn't them but a reflection of various elements of them used for business, their apprehension generally diminishes.

It is useful to examine examples such as Lady Gaga, who has a brilliant online brand, with almost 40 million Twitter followers, nearly 60 million likes on Facebook and a very high level of engagement from her fans. Lady Gaga is really Stefani Joanne Angelina Germanotta, and the person under the outrageous clothes and publicity stunts, I am sure, is remarkably different from her pop star persona. Of course, we don't know what she is really like because her online interactions with the public are largely via social networking and other media. As savvy as she is in the use of digital branding, we only see the elements of her personality that are congruent with her brand. That said, she is authentic – you can feel it – and this is what resonates with her fans. She puts so much of herself out there and her public loves her for it. Yet she still maintains a level of secrecy around her private life. Very clever. So the lesson is: be real, but choose what you share of your inner self. You don't have to reveal everything.

The third potential pitfall is that people will inevitably judge you and your brand instantly based on the pictures and text that you choose to represent yourself with. One of the reasons Facebook has been so popular is that it is based on pictures, and people immediately making judgements based on them. This is why it is incredibly important that your profile photo on Facebook is authentic, and preferably taken by a professional photographer, which will be explained further later in the book. Still, it's normal that not everyone will appreciate your online Personal Brand. In fact, as we have discussed, this can be useful as it weeds out the clients you don't really want so that you can focus your energy on clients who are a better fit for what you do.

I feel you getting nervous now, but fear not. Keep reading, as the challenge of getting ready to promote yourself authentically online is balanced by the substantial rewards of a successful brand. Your Personal Brand is like a bank account. The more authentic, transparent and individual you are, the more dollars you add to your account, which you can then trade for cash. If you keep your claims and statements real, you don't deplete personal capital. Then you will keep accumulating profit and also get interest.

Are you ready to create your Personal Brand? Great, let's get started!

CHAPTER 4

Understand Yourself

'When your values are clear to you, making decisions becomes easier.'
Roy Disney

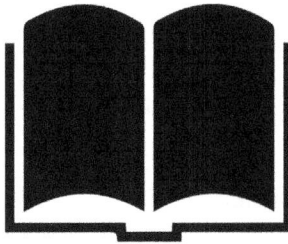

The first step to creating a strong Personal Brand is to understand the person behind the brand. Before you jump right in and make your website and post in social media, it is important to sit back and reflect on what exactly you are going to talk about and how you are going to position yourself in the market. This section will challenge you to dig deep, think about your brand and consider some useful tools to help you along the way.

'Know thyself' is an often-quoted adage and, like most statements that have stood the test of time, this one is a golden rule of success. The problem is that it is difficult to see yourself objectively because you are in your own head 24/7, 365 days a year, without an opportunity to step outside yourself to critically analyse how you are made up. Therefore, it is vital to undergo personality testing and other similar tests to gain an objective perspective on your personality and traits.

In my first meeting with new clients I spend the initial hour listening to them and asking specific questions to find out what the essence of them and their brand is. I ask questions like:

- What do you want?
- What do you love to do?
- If money were no concern, what would you do with your time?
- What do you daydream about when you are supposed to be working?
- What are your goals, and what do you want to achieve?

These questions get clients thinking about what they really love to do, without worrying about how it relates to their business. Sometimes clients don't see the relevance of this part of the conversation until I reveal the greater strategy, and then an 'a-ha!' moment occurs and the light bulb comes on. In fact, this is one of the reasons I love to help people with their brands and businesses: to see the instant when they shift their thinking and can see the opportunities for themselves that I do, perceive themselves as the world does, and feel inspired in their businesses again.

Let's start with some questions to begin your process of self-discovery. Who are you? I mean, who are you really, deep down? What do you like to do and what do you hate? What personality type are you and how do you work best? What do you want now and what are you realistically able to achieve? It is absolutely key to know the answers to these questions before constructing a Personal Business and Brand. Your business needs to be congruent with you or it will not meet the criteria for a Personal Business and will struggle to take advantage of the benefits of attraction marketing.

It is no use me giving a brilliantly designed strategy to a new client if the person doesn't execute it. Likewise, there's no point in executing a strategy if it doesn't fulfil the needs of a business. A strategy must fit the individual's style and preferred work behaviours for it to be carried through passionately and successfully.

I have asked all the above questions above of myself and tested all my theories and methodologies on my own brand. I have also completed all the tests I talk about in this section, so I know what works for me and what doesn't. I understand my values, my personality and how I work in teams. It's my firm belief that doing this work sets a robust foundation for your brand. Let's now explore these things in more detail.

GOALS

What do you want? What are you trying to achieve with your work? What really fulfils you? These are all important questions, and the more you drill down on the answer, the more you will be able to construct a Personal Business to really suit your needs. It is no use creating a business in which you will not be inspired to get up and work each day. When you truly understand yourself and can create a business around this, you will not require external motivation to do it, you will be internally inspired as it matches your deepest values and fulfils you. List below your top six goals for your business, and then review them at the end of the section to see if they have changed.

Top six goals:

1.
2.
3.
4.
5.
6.

Your goals are based upon what you want in life, and are a representation of your values. Let's discover more about your values and see how they affect your goals.

VALUES

What are your values? I am not talking about Ten Commandment–type values such as 'Thou shall not lie', but rather, what you truly think is important and what makes you happiest. Not what you think you ought to believe or what society or others say is right, but your own specific and honest values. The branch of science devoted to understanding values is known as *axiology*. As humans, we share many universal traits with one another; however, we still each follow our own path in life based on what is most important to us. That is, according to our values.

Have you ever felt that your partner or boss just didn't understand you? Didn't 'get' why a certain thing you wanted was extremely important to you and just disregarded it like it was nothing at all? Well, that's a difference in values. There is great benefit in knowing not just your own value hierarchy, but also those of the people around you. Wouldn't it be useful if you could understand what is most important to your partner, boss or customers – what makes them tick – and could then find a way to link your values to theirs? Sure it would! The first step is to understand your own.

The good news is that you already know your values. You may not have consciously noticed them, but you can see them in your life if you look hard enough. For instance, consider how you spend your time. There will always be things you have to do, but there will be other things that you choose to do and will always make time for. These are the things that you really love, which, of course, will reflect your highest values.

For example, I can always squeeze in an exercise session. I'll have a quick run before dinner, or get up a little earlier so I can go to the gym. Perhaps I'll be a few minutes late to see a friend so I can go for a swim, or I'll even do a yoga session with a client to fulfil two of my values. I extend my busy schedule to fit in exercise because I love it and it supports the high value I place on health and longevity.

Exercise, however, is not my business: consulting and educating are. But I don't feel guilty when I spend time fulfilling the value I put on health because I realise that a healthy body helps me in my business. To be able to work hard and maintain a high-energy output is important when I am building businesses and dealing with clients. Keeping fit also relates to one of my other core values: my children. I want to be able to climb a tree, kick a football and go skiing with them. Showing them the value of health and vitality through teaching by example is part of my strategy. So far it works, as my three year old can now do five chin-ups and my seven year old even more! Not because I told them to do it, but because I put a chin-up bar in my house and they see me use it and want to be like Daddy. Monkey see, monkey do. Unfortunately, the same cannot be said for seeing me eat vegetables instead of lollies, but that's another story ...

The awakening of my true values and knowing what I really love to do occurred when I was introduced to Dr John Demartini, a well-known American writer, researcher and teacher. I was fortunate to meet him over lunch before I knew much about his work and then saw him on stage straight after – his speech was awe-inspiring to me. His teachings in axiology are the best I have seen and I recommend you review his work – specifically, his book *Inspired Destiny*, which details the full process of how to discover your mission and values in life. You can purchase this book via my website, www.andrewford.com.au/resources. He is an amazing man and he doesn't just stop at a greater understanding of who we are and what drives us to do the things we do, he has also created a body of work to explain the workings of the entire universe! I kid you not. So although we will only review values in this book, I encourage you to read more about Dr Demartini.

It's also essential to understand how values interrelate. Central to all my values is my business. I love what I do and every day I feel grateful for my clients and the people I work with. I feel fortunate that I love my work and that I have been able to construct it around my values. My business supports my children and myself, it provides me social outlets with my clients and colleagues, and it gives me freedom to fit exercise in when I feel like it. All of my core values support each other.

This doesn't mean that your career will be based on everything you love. As discussed, I love my two boys and spend a lot of time with them on holidays and weekends. I am quite passionate about coffee – making my own and appreciating the rich smell and taste of an amazing latte. I also love skiing, beer and the beach, but none of this means that I want to be a ski instructor full time, a bartender or a personal trainer. However, any business I pursue has to take into account that I have young children, so I can't be away from home for long periods and need flexibility in my working hours. What's more, I make sure that I can fit work in with exercise and taking the time to enjoy the small things, such as a good coffee. It's vital to understand your main values and to find a way for them to intertwine.

So what does this have to do with constructing a Personal Business? Everything! Your brand is all about what you love, your energy and the way you want to work – and the more you express these things in your brand, the more you will attract opportunities that reflect your values. For example, I have had many business opportunities present themselves on ski trips, while doing swims and fun runs, or while playing with the kids in the park, all of which are activities that support my values. People buy from like-minded people and want to find common ground between their values and your own. I often meet people for business and if we get onto a topic that we are both passionate about and where our values meet, the conversation become more synergised, we have rapport and we *find* ways to work together.

There are seven core areas of life: family, friends, money, career, health, spirituality and education. Order these areas of life, your values, in the table on the next page. Remember, they can change with your circumstances, but it's still vital to be aware of what they are during different phases in your life.

It is important to order the list according what you actually feel, not what you think others will like; there are no right or wrong results. You are a unique individual and wonderful exactly the way you are, so please don't tailor your information just to seem like a better parent, worker or spouse. Be honest in your answers and you will discover that when you live a life true to your values and in a way that matches your personality and strengths, it opens up a much more fulfilling existence. One of my favourite quotes from Dr Demartini is that he would rather the world be pissed at him, than for him to be pissed at himself. Never have truer words been spoken, because if you bow to the pressures of others to be something you are not, there will always be tension, and you will subconsciously work your way back to your values whether you notice it or not!

VALUE	WRITE WHERE YOU DEMONSTRATE THIS IN YOUR LIFE (TIME, MONEY, ATTENTION)	CURRENT RANK 1–7
Family		
Friends		
Money		
Career		
Health		
Spirituality		
Education		

Once you understand your values and their priority in your life, you can create your Personal Business to reflect them and ensure they are met, otherwise you will unconsciously sabotage yourself in order to get back to your real values. I have seen this often with clients. They say they want financial wealth, when their lives don't reflect that, and with some work they realise they have all the wealth they desire in their health, family, friends or education. They are striving for a false goal; if they focused on what they really wanted, instead of what they see as society's values, they would actually have a more successful business and more financial wealth! Crazy but true.

If your business reflects your values, customers and partners will see the authenticity in your business and want to help you, promote you and help with your attraction marketing. The connection with your clients will be stronger, as they match your values, and they'll be happier paying your fees and be more likely to be repeat clients over time.

PERSONALITY TESTING

It's likely that your values will be strongly influenced by your personality. I truly believe that people pop out into this world very much like they will end up as adults. When you have children, you realise that your kids have very distinct personalities right from day one. Unlike values, which change over time, your personality is somewhat fixed. So it is beneficial to have a good understanding of your personality, because it affects many elements of how you want to represent your brand and how you can operate it in digital media. One great way to do this is with personality testing.

Doing personality testing can help you to become crystal clear about how you can perform at your best. It defines how you perceive the world and the way you digest information. There are a multitude of personality tests and I have completed quite a few because of all the years I spent working in large corporations. Large companies, particularly American ones, love these types of tests as they provide valuable knowledge about where individuals are best suited to work in the hierarchy structure. Unfortunately, in my experience of doing these tests – some of which involved full three-day courses – once a test was completed, there was no follow-up by the company. My advice is to do the test and use the results, as they are a gift. I gained fantastic insight into my psychology and personality, which has assisted me in developing my Personal Business to complement the way I am.

If you are an employee, these tests can also assist you in getting the role you most want. In today's business environment, workers are more independent and need to manage themselves and their careers, so you might not get an opportunity to do the tests at work. Having some knowledge of your personality in a clearly defined way can really help you negotiate your role to best suit what you love most. For instance, if a manager has a strong visionary profile but lacks the detail to make the vision run smoothly, and your core skills are in the detail, you're a match! Especially if you can demonstrate it with a report that is clearly articulated.

Personality testing can also help you select a different workplace if your current one doesn't match your values. But it isn't just about you, it is also useful for your team. If you are a small business owner or entrepreneur, it can help you understand the people and resources you will need around you to fill the gaps in your own work behaviour, be that via hiring partners, staff or contractors to do the jobs you aren't suited to.

Myers-Briggs

The most popular test is the Myers-Briggs personality test, which was based on the principles of Carl Jung, one of the fathers of modern psychology. In his 1921 book *Psychological Types*, he theorised that people experience the world through four filters: sensation, intuition, feeling and thinking. I know I am an ESTJ, and this tells me some great information regarding my personality. However, I find the information too general and not specific enough about business. Therefore, I recommend Roger Hamilton's Wealth Dynamics as it is specifically designed to show how our personality can generate the most value for our businesses.

Wealth Dynamics

This test is geared towards helping you generate wealth, but it is also a broader measure of business traits. Hamilton's test can be found via my website www.socialstar.com.au/resources; I recommend you do the test now. My results categorised me in the *Creator* profile, which means that my primary focus in business is coming up with new ideas and that I am most fulfilled when working with others to brainstorm this vision. This profile was very accurate for me, and I knew from doing other personality tests that the results were accurate. I gained a great deal of insight from the detailed description of how to best use this profile to ensure success in business and creative value for the world and also wealth. I recommend that you check out Hamilton's work, as he is truly a leader in his field.

The Wealth Dynamics assessment will also bring to the surface a lot of the challenges your personality type may face when generating wealth. Every personality type has benefits and drawbacks, so be prepared to see and understand this balance. It isn't good or bad, it just is, so to overcome these barriers to your success I recommend seeking a business mentor or coach who can assist in developing strategies to ensure you're focusing on your strengths and creating plans to mitigate your challenges.

INTELLIGENCE TESTING

One of the areas underpinning our ability in business is our intelligence, both intellectual and emotional. Therefore, the next phase of understanding yourself is to know your intelligence and strengths.

Having a high intelligence is not necessarily a leading contributor to somebody succeeding in business, making money or a leading a fulfilled life. In fact, some of the most financially successful of my friends are the least 'intelligent' from an intelligence quotient (IQ) or educational perspective. Of course, not being academically minded does preclude certain careers. For example, if you want to be a lawyer or doctor you need a certain intelligence level to successfully complete the study. However, even in those fields, intelligence alone will not ensure success, as hard work and persistence often play crucial roles in success!

Some careers require a higher IQ than others, some require a higher emotional quotient (EQ), and others call for a combination of both. One thing I do know is that having knowledge about your IQ – the breakdown of where it is strongest and where it is weaker, more than the overall number – can assist you in honing your direction in life.

I completed an intelligence test after I had just left high school and was feeling lost in my career. I was working in a warehouse, partying a lot, not looking after my health, and focusing on social activities that were not furthering me in life. I was going nowhere fast, but didn't care, as I was having a great time! I was young, and I'd been told during my school years that I wasn't very smart so I wasn't aspiring to more.

Fortunately, my mother thought I had more ability so she sent me to get an intelligence test. The results shocked me. I was especially astounded as I went into the test hung-over, late and with little confidence that I would be anything more than average. I discovered that I was not average, as I had believed; in fact, I was in the 'superior intelligence' section with the top 6.7 per cent of the population. My suitable job roles were things I had thought were out of my grasp at school: a surgeon, university lecturer or judge. My score was 127 out of 150 – only two marks from 'genius' level. Imagine if I hadn't gone out until 3 a.m. the night before partying! I also found that I was balanced in the different areas of intelligence, having strong traits in emotional intelligence.

I cannot understate how profound this test was for my confidence and how it affected my future. The test changed my perspective, gave me confidence to do more with my life. I started to study, tentatively at first, but as my confidence grew I took on greater and more advanced challenges. I have now fulfilled my potential within my value of education, and it was all spurred on by a test that proved I had some ability in that area. The test didn't give me anything more than a realistic understanding of my capabilities and some confidence. It wasn't someone's opinion, it was objective, and that was key to me. The results motivated me to pursue opportunities for further education that I otherwise might not have undertaken.

I chose to apply myself, studying before and after work and missing out on social occasions to achieve my goal. It was hard work, but I saw education as my route to a more successful life. Education became high on my list of values, and more important than drinking, being social or watching TV. As I transformed one area of my life, the flow-on effects to my confidence meant that I became more productive in other areas. I developed a lifelong love of exercise, started to save and invest my money and had more rewarding relationships.

While not everybody will achieve a high overall result on an intelligence test, everyone will see strengths in certain areas of intelligence. If you find out what you are suited to, it will give you more confidence to pursue the areas where you excel and to set new goals. Everyone has unique abilities and skills, and knowing what they are is important to constructing a Personal Business upon these foundations.

STRENGTHS AND WEAKNESSES

There are two schools of thought regarding strengths. The first is that you should work on your weaknesses to make them stronger. The second is that you should focus purely on your strengths. I subscribe to the second theory and believe that when you are working to your strengths you're more likely to be success-ful. Think of Olympic athletes, they dedicate themselves to one task: to be the best. Sure, they cross train, but their mission is purely focused around one activity they want to be successful at. They harness all their resources around one activity and the more focused they are, the more likely they will succeed.

The first step to understanding your strengths and weak-nesses is to list them in priority order from 1 to 6. Articulating them will help to clarify what they are, and it is possible for others to review and confirm your selection.

Top six strengths:

1.
2.
3.
4.
5.
6.

Top six weaknesses:

1.
2.
3.
4.
5.
6.

Once you have written down your strengths and perceived weaknesses, you can focus your time on building up your strengths to be your unique differentiator and seek assistance in outsourcing or getting systems to support the areas that are weaknesses.

Please don't confuse strengths with values or personality traits. Values are areas of life that we prioritise based on what's important to us, and personality traits are our preferences for dealing with the world and interpreting information though our senses. Strengths are what we are naturally good at. The kicker is that we will normally be strong in areas that are important to us and relate to our personality traits. For example, I enjoy public speaking. It is a common fear among many people, but not for me – I love it. Why? I put a high value on business and presenting is a great way to connect to many people at once, so it is connected to one of my highest values. I am an extrovert in my Myers-Biggs personality assessment and a Creator/Star in Wealth Dynamics, which both point to a desire to spend time with people and particularly be the centre of attention. Finally, I have been practising speaking for over a decade and believe I have some skills in this area. I like it because I believe I am good at it.

It wasn't always this way. At school I hated speaking and it wasn't until I was working at Hewlett-Packard and my job demanded a lot of speaking that I developed my skills in that area. However, once I had confidence in my skills, I loved it! I have now been on stages all over the world, speaking at major conferences in different languages in front of hundreds of people and really enjoying it. It has become a strength and because of that, I want to do more of it. So instead of focusing my energy developing one of my weaknesses, I will focus on getting even better at public speaking.

YOUR RELATIONSHIPS WITH OTHERS

Knowing more about yourself and how you operate is important, however, we don't operate a Personal Business in a vacuum so it is important to see how we are going to operate our business in relationship to others. The first area is teamwork and the second is in relation to your life stage.

Teamwork

We are all dependent on others when we work and if we do not understand how we prefer to interact with others given our different strengths and values, often there will be conflict and poor results.

The team personality test I like to use is called the Life Styles Inventory by Human Synergistics. It's a behavioural model that examines your personality as others see it. The test reviews three different behaviour styles: Constructive Styles, Passive/ Defensive Styles and Aggressive/Defensive Styles. It then breaks these down into twelve specific thinking and behaviour styles.

I completed this assessment with my team at Sensis and it was very interesting for them and myself. My profile result was mostly in the *Constructive* area, which was not surprising to me as it matched the other personality tests I had completed. However, it was revealing to see the results of my management team, as their behaviours were more at the *Aggressive* end of the spectrum. The interesting outcome (or lack thereof) from the assessment was no changes were made to staff members roles as a result of the assessment. If you're running a company, my advice is to have you and your staff undertake assessment to find out how you all work in teams, but ensure that you make use of the results to place people in the right areas. Staff generally want to do a good job, and they will work best when their values are engaged and they are in a role that suits their natural personality.

If you work within a team environment or planning on creating one, this is a very useful tool and one about which I suggest you seek out more information.

YOUR LIFE STAGE

The life stage you are at right now will significantly affect the way you set up your Personal Business. By life stage, I am referring to the major changes in life such as children, marriage, studies, illness, retirement and other things that can dramatically alter your values and the way you run your business. The impact of these events will vary depending on your values and personality and what type of business you operate, but it is useful to document your plans to ensure you are setting yourself up for success.

For instance, children are one of life's blessings, and they also have a significant impact on business, particularly for women. I have two young boys, so I understand how much energy they take to raise. My eldest boy didn't sleep through the night for four years! Imagine going to work each day, studying at night, when you are up every single night looking after your baby. It is quite frankly debilitating. But you survive and it is amazing how you cope with these changes.

The changes my family made after having two children was that my wife stopped working full time and I worked harder to climb the corporate ladder and earn more money. However, this clashed with my value of being an active, hands-on dad, so I was torn. I wanted to see my kids grow up, and that's when I made serious plans to start my own business so I could spend more time with my kids and keep my business ambitions on track. The solution wasn't to work less; it was to have more flexibility in my work. My wife didn't work for eighteen months for each child, which had an impact on her career progression, however, that was a choice that we made based on our shared values. The next life stage I am planning for is when both of my children are at school, and I want to be able to take more time off during school holidays to be with them.

My recommendation for you is to plan your next ten years of your business, taking into account all that you have learnt regarding values and life stages. If you are planning a family and place a high value on spending time with your kids, don't build a Personal Business around your time! Build it around your product or service and allow others to run your business while you are looking after the family.

BE REALISTIC

Undertaking psychological and professional testing literally changed my life – that's why I encourage you to learn more about yourself. You will be surprised by what you find and it will give you the tools to construct your Personal Business and brand in an authentic way. You may discover that you are working towards goals that are really not in line with your true values. There may be important aspects of your personality or key strengths that you haven't been taking advantage of and using in your career. It is important that we understand ourselves and what our path in life is, as many of us have dreams for greatness that are built on fantasy prescribed from media and others. It is important to be realistic.

I do not hold the belief that a person can do anything they want. Yes, we all have potential to have a fulfilling life and we can achieve greatness, but there are physical, financial and situational barriers that hinder our progression to having *anything* we want. Take for instance the myriad of TV talent shows, such as *The Voice* and *The X Factor*. They are all a contest and only one person can win, so if all the contestants have the dream of winning, 99.99 per cent of them will not fulfil their dream. The same goes for every sporting contest, be it the Olympics, the Rugby World Cup or a boxing title. The same also applies in business, wealth, health and all areas of life. There are those at the top of the list, and the vast majority are in the middle or at the bottom.

How disappointing, you may think. I am not trying to kill your dreams. I want your dreams to be based on what is really important for you, and not on things that are unrealistic fantasies – that would be setting yourself up for failure. Once you are aware of your highest values, your personality profile and your strengths, you can set goals knowing what you really want to be fulfilled as a unique and amazing individual. That is real fulfilment.

For instance, my goals are to help people find their path via their business, be financially independent, spend time with my boys, keep fit and be the best man I can be. I have been working on this all my adult life without even knowing it! I don't set myself unrealistic dreams, such as win this or that competition or have this much money. My fulfilment isn't based on these achievements as I feel gratitude for my life as it is now, while working towards more growth in all areas of my life. Therefore, it isn't the achievement of goals that I believe makes the difference; it is the *choice* of goals. You can't control the external circumstances, so work on growing yourself and accept all the learnings and challenges as steps in the process, and you will be fulfilled now.

This is the good news. You automatically attract skills around your values as they are what you love doing; you will find if you look that you probably have amassed amazing resources for your Personal Business, without consciously trying. I have seen dozens of clients who thought their résumé was a disparate mix of roles and once I connected the dots for them, they saw the perfection in their lives and the flow of energy to their new mission. They had everything they needed to start their Personal Business, but hadn't understood themselves or their path clearly enough to begin. All they required was a spark and a little clarity.

Early in this chapter we listed our top six goals. Now we will revise them to see if they have altered after completing our Understanding assessments. Write down your top goals once more. Revised top six goals:

1.

2.

3.

4.

5.

6.

Are your goals the same or have they changed? There is no right or wrong. Your goals are a statement of intent for the future and are very important to write down regularly as they can and should change, based on new information and your own growth. Simply having a goal starts the process in your mind to achieve what you have stated you wish to achieve. Be careful what you wish for, as you might just get it!

Truly knowing yourself is critical to completing the next phase, of understanding where your brand is now and then constructing your Personal Brand, so ensure you have completed this section thoroughly before continuing onto the next chapter.

CHAPTER 5

Where is Your Brand Now?

'An unexamined life is not worth living.'
Socrates

In the next phase of constructing your Personal Business, you will focus primarily on where your Personal Brand is now. As discussed, your Personal Brand is the main way to create an attraction marketing campaign, which uses your online presence as the main feature. Therefore, we will start by reviewing your current online brand and how the public sees you. Then we will run through a process to uncover what you really want your brand to be, and finally, we'll document the new brand so we can start building it.

LOOKING INTO THE GOOGLE MIRROR

'Googling yourself' has become a mandatory pastime for social media–savvy people wanting to know how they are perceived in the digital world. However, you will require professional help to do a detailed examination, understand the results and know how to influence the outcome. Social Star specialises in completing rigorous Digital Diagnoses for our clients and, for the first time, I will now unveil how we do it and reveal practical strategies to influence your results.

As you do the searches I'm about to list, take a screen capture of each result and paste it into a PowerPoint document for comparison later in the book. This document is your Digital Diagnosis record.

I recommend that you start by googling yourself and looking at the first three pages of results, or more if nothing shows up in those initial results. What you are looking for is any mention of your name in social media – such as websites, LinkedIn, Facebook, Twitter, blogs, Google+, news articles and so on – links on others websites, the pages of current and previous workplaces, and others who have mentioned you.

The way Google currently works is to find the most relevant result for the person searching. It takes into account where the search is conducted, if it is a mobile device or big screen, the URL and content on the page, links to the page and how long it has been in existence for. Google is always tinkering with the search algorithm so instead of trying to be a SEO specialist, I would just try to make your information as specific as you can be in relation to what your clients are looking for. This is a great reason to have a personal website as it is the most specific result for your name. For Andrew Ford I have www.andrewford.com.au, which is a very relevant result for people searching on my name, particularly in Australia, as it is a .au domain. I usually display second behind another Andrew Ford. I wasn't able to secure the .com URL so for international searches on my profile I will have a lower result than in Australia. I highly recommend that my clients purchase their name in a URL from a reliable provider such as GoDaddy. For more details and a link to GoDaddy, see my website, www.andrewford.com.au/resources.

It is important to not just see where you are listed, but to also notice who else comes up around your name. If your name is uncommon then there might be very few people competing for that search result. If your name is common (like mine) then there could be several people competing for space on social media and other sites. You can't move other people but you definitely change your ranking by using some smart techniques, but more on that later.

Notice also the search engine marketing (SEM) results on the top and right-hand side of the page. Are there any? If so, what are they advertising? For my name, Andrew Ford, a common search result for SEM is Ford cars. If people are advertising against your name they are paying each time someone clicks on it based on the Google AdWords auction system; this is what SEM is all about. Another feature you might see is a box on the right-hand side featuring a photo, description and other rich content for a person. This is from Wikipedia and is a really strong addition to your profile, as Google particularly ranks this information highly because it is independent. You can only get a Wikipedia profile if you are a person 'of note' so it isn't for everyone, mainly celebrities. For more on Wikipedia see the social media section.

Once you've completed a thorough Google search, repeat the process with other search engines, such as Yahoo, Bing and your local country sites, as the unique algorithms of each site will yield different results. Another useful practice is to search from another computer, or to clear your 'cookies', as search engines track your browsing behaviour, which means you might see different results from one computer to another.

After completing a search on your name, follow the same process with your aliases. This is particularly important if you are known under a different name, such as a nickname or a previous marriage surname, or you have names in different languages such as a Chinese name and an English one.

Once you've compiled all your screen captures in a PowerPoint document, you're ready to move on to the next step, which is picture searching. Conduct the same searches but in 'image' mode if you are using Google or another search engine. Notice where you are placed compared to others and hover over the pictures to see the website source, so that if you want to remove it you know where it is from. For example, if a blogger featured a story and picture of you and it consistently ranks highly, you could ask them if you can write a follow-up article.

All of this self-examination is a vital step to understanding where your current ranking is when searching on your name in popular search engines. As discussed earlier, there are only three ways for clients to find you: your name, your business and your service, and since we are constructing a Personal Business based on your Personal Brand, it is essential to have a high ranking on your name in search engines.

Believe me, people *will* look you up – it is more common than you may think. To see exactly how many people are searching for your name, use the free Google AdWords Keyword Planner and simply type in your name and location, and it will show you the volume of searches in the last month or year. How awesome is Google for providing free tools like this! Cut and paste this into your Digital Diagnosis record as well.

Finally, search within all of your social media sites, such as Facebook, Twitter, LinkedIn, Instagram, Google+, Pinterest and any other site you are on. Remember to review any past sites, such as MySpace or PhotoBucket, that you may no longer use, as they could still show up in certain results. These sites may or may not come up on a general search, but if there is content associated with your name it will appear somewhere, so it's best to be thorough.

Now you have completed the big screen search, it is time to do the same on your mobile phone. In most countries mobile internet traffic is overtaking the big screen, hence the need to replicate all the searches on your mobile device to ensure you understand the differences in placement in the different environments. Take screen captures with your device and import the pictures to your computer and, you guessed it, put it into your Digital Diagnosis for your records.

WHAT DOES YOUR BRAND SAY ABOUT YOU?

Once you have assembled your Digital Diagnosis presentation it is time to review how you appear to others. Wait a few days and then review the file with some colleagues you trust. Ask them to consider how they would perceive your Personal Brand if they didn't know you. Be sure not to hide things from them that you don't want to share. Be open to their comments and perceptions, as you need to know what others honestly think. If you don't, how can you make changes?

The goal of reviewing the Digital Diagnosis is to narrow down the key words and pictures that currently represent your online brand to people who don't know you. I completed my first review of myself in November 2011, early in the Social Star business years. The results were pretty clear, and not particularly good. I was using a different photo in every social media site, had limited followers and had a low level of engagement from my community. It was a sporadic brand, to say the least. It was perceived as creative and dynamic, but shallow and lacking substance. My photos showed someone trying a bit too hard to gain attention with crazy stunts rather than quality work. The question that emerged from the review was this: how do I want to be perceived?

To figure out what I wanted my Personal Brand to be, I decided to use some of the techniques I had developed when reviewing company brands. The first step for you to adopt these techniques involves creating mood boards – one with words and one with images. The word board will assist you in coming up with the appropriate words for your online presence. Begin by listing the four traits you think represent you best. Positive descriptive terms such as 'outgoing', 'friendly', 'hardworking' and 'enthusiastic' are useful.

Top four positive traits:

1.
2.
3.
4.

You should also consider four negative traits you believe you have, as these too will be part of your brand. Terms such as 'lack of detail', 'pessimistic', 'short attention span' and 'frugal' could be used. The reason we need to explore both sides of your personality is that your clients and potential customers may see these sides as well.

Top four negative traits:

1.
2.
3.
4.

We will not use these negative traits in your brand, but we may need to negate them in your online presence. If you have a reputation for lacking in detail, for instance, we could negate that on your website by mentioning upfront that details are managed by outsourcing this task to a colleague or process. There may also be an opportunity to show specific attention to detail in certain blog posts to counteract the reputation. Furthermore, when you talk to clients you could also reassure them by saying, 'Oh, sometimes I lack some detail so it is great to have John to check all my documentation before I send it out.'

This raises an important point in your branding. You are all things to your clients – both positive and negative sides to their solution. There is always a balance in every person and every service. For instance, the best person for the job might also be the most costly and the most in-demand and hard to book. On the flipside, a lesser-known person might be cheap and readily available, but they could be inefficient and lack clarity in their work. Your customer is always looking at both sides, so bring up their concerns for them. If you only mention the positives, they will go looking for or simply imagine what the negatives are. So do the work for them and present it in a way that achieves their goals.

For example, if you are the best at what you do and are considerably more expensive than the competition, don't hide your prices until the end of a negotiation with a client and surprise them with the cost. Tell them upfront that you are the most valued operator in your field and that you charge accordingly. Demonstrate your worth in the way you present your brand, and make it clear that you are in demand and have to schedule clients well in advance and that only seriously interested customers need apply. Don't offend anyone or be arrogant, but do be authentic. If you are the best, be the best. Acknowledge it and your clients will appreciate it. You will spend less time with people who are not your perfect client because they can't afford you or want something different. Don't leave it until the job is agreed upon for both of you to discover that you are an inappropriate match.

Once you have listed your eight traits, choose one that you could say most represents you. If a positive trait was 'outgoing' and the negative was 'short attention span', think of how you would like your clients to perceive you. It can help to imagine a scenario where a client may perceive either a negative or positive trait. For example, if you met them at a function and you were engaging and socialising with them at the start, then shook their hand, gave them your business card and quickly moved on, they might think of you as shallow or uncaring of their needs, or they could perceive you as busy and in demand. Therefore, the optimal trait for this situation could be desired or popular, whatever you feel fits you best. Consider the one word that would describe your optimal brand perception and write this below.

Optimal Trait _____

Now that we have one trait, we need to repeat the above process with pictures. So start with a blank sheet of paper, or a PowerPoint slide, and write in the corners your top four positive traits. The reason we start with words is because these can help us find appropriate pictures via a Google image search. Type in the words you brainstormed on the trait chart – both negative and positive – and see what images Google throws at you.

By the way, when I say negative and positive, I use these terms because people will generally understand what I mean and apply it to the way they see themselves. However, most traits are not actually negative or positive – they are neutral until someone judges them via their values. 'Frugal', for instance, can be a perceived as a positive trait if you're an accountant and saving a client money, or a negative trait if you're an accountant and not providing dynamic investment advice. The accountant is neither good nor bad – it is the values of the client that determines the judgement.

This is why having a very specific Personal Brand is so vital to find clients who match your values and therefore see your strongest traits as positive or beneficial to them. Think about this concept and apply it to your business situation before moving on, as it is a very, very powerful idea. You may have worked with clients in the past whom there was no pleasing, no matter what you did. It was not their fault or yours; it was almost certainly a clash of values caused by a loose Personal Brand and non-specific understanding of yourself at the start of the process. But I digress ...

Continue to google pictures related to the traits on your trait chart and remember that the images don't have to be of people or specific objects – they can be of anything that resonates with you emotionally. They will not be used directly in your website or online brand – they are to inform you of what your core brand is and the type of imaging that you feel best represents what you are trying to achieve. Follow the same process with all the traits in the chart until you have one core picture at the centre of the page that you feel really captures your essence.

If you are having trouble finding images that you think really represent you, there's another process that usually helps. I use this technique with clients who need to project the process onto another person to access their true awareness of themselves. I ask them to list the people in their field whom they most respect and admire. They will usually select people who work in fields in which their values are important or people with whom they share similar attributes. People generally like and respect successful people who they see as being similar to them, however, they might not believe that they can be like their heroes, so they resist comparing themself to them.

Once they have a few names, I get them to search for these people in Google Images to see what appears, and what feelings come from those images. These will be the desired visual representations of the client, which they were perhaps too shy or embarrassed to consider for themselves. This process can be quite powerful in revealing how you really want to be perceived.

Once you've found the ideal words and images that represent you, we will use them to guide the next phase in your branding, which is the *doing* phase. Finding the right text and visuals for your brand is vital for very specific reasons. The digital world is built on words and pictures. Search engines can only read words – they can't see pictures or interpret images – so we need to be specific in how we want to be represented.

The challenge in Personal Branding isn't so much having clients understand themselves as they intuitively know what they like and don't like. The issue arises when they try to articulate this to other people in words and pictures. This is the reason we worked through the *Understand* section in so much detail – it assists the client to be very clear on their brand but also provides important information to their branding team, to articulate exactly what the client's brand is. This is also the purpose of the Digital Diagnosis and the mood boards we have just created; they all form part of the brief you can give a brand designer, website builder and social media creator. The better your briefs, the better your brand work will be!

The dilemma with digital branding is that although the internet is only built on words, humans prefer images over words. In fact, people are becoming more visual as time goes on, so you will find that websites and social media contain fewer words and more video and pictures as people become more time-poor and have higher volumes of data to sift through. Therefore, it's essential to understand your brand from both a computing and human perspective.

Now, on to the action of actually creating your Personal Brand!

CHAPTER 6

Build Your Assets

*'The best time to plant a tree was 20 years ago.
The second best time is now.'*
Chinese Proverb

To create your Personal Brand the way that I do at Social Star requires many elements, so this section is particularly long. We usually assess clients early in the process and only teach them the online tools they need in order to operate their brands effectively. We have completed most of this thinking and work for them, so they don't need to know about every digital option out there – we have discussed, advised and agreed on the best ones for that particular client. All client needs are different.

Later in this chapter, we will review all the main platforms you might need at the time of writing so you can make your own assessment of what is best for your particular Personal Brand. You can simply read the ones pertinent to you and skip the others for a later time if you desire. For example, if you really hate Twitter as a channel and have no intention of using it, you might focus instead on another that particularly appeals to you, such as LinkedIn. If so, just read the LinkedIn section and once you have created your site you can review the others when you have more time and scope to take on a new challenge.

YOUR NAME

The first and most basic – yet important – step of creating your Personal Brand is deciding what you are going to call yourself. Of course, this might seem a strange step for some, as your name is your name. However, you may be bilingual and have names in different languages. Or if you have been married you might have changed your name. You might have a nickname or alias, as some professional artists do, which better represents you than your real name. Whatever the situation, you need to decide on a name that best suits the new brand you wish to create. It will be used on your personal website and in all of your social media channels. And while it can be changed later, it is best to carefully consider your choice before starting the process.

The review of your current name will assist you in making this decision. My first name is Andrew, but most people call me Andy, and as I want to appear more accessible and friendly, I choose to use the latter in some of my social media. The issue for me is that both Andrew and Andy Ford are very common names, so on Twitter, that name and any derivative I could think of were already taken. So I had to make up a new name, and the handle @SirFord was born. This might seem a strange alternative when I wanted to be less formal to my clients, but some of them call me Mr Ford as a sign of respect in a fun way. Therefore, that seemed to suit my brand. Twitter also shows my real name on the page, and as most people use an unusual handle on the site anyway, it worked for me.

Once you have your name finalised – and a few backups prepared in case it's already taken on various social media – you need to buy the URL. The best URL you can get is www. yourname.com, but also buy the one for your local country, so for Australia it is www.yourname.com.au. If this isn't available, try for www.yourname.net or any of the other recommended varieties. There are so many variations to choose from and they are inexpensive, so buy a few. You can easily change the URL your website points to and even have several URLs pointing to the one website if required. I have more details on GoDaddy on my website, at www.andrewford.com. au/resources.

Once you have a URL to house your Personal Brand, you will need a website to use as a base for your brand.

PERSONAL WEBSITES

A personal website is one that represents you and your brand. As discussed, it is different from your business or company website as the URL should contain your name. Once you have a URL you need to find a provider who will host your website. Think of it like you have a jacket (website) that you want to hang up, so you get a coat hanger (URL) and put it in your cupboard (host provider). You may buy your URL from your host, but you don't have to.

Before creating your site, there is a bit of technical stuff you need to do – such as pointing the Domain Name System (DNS) server towards the URL – so get a friend who knows about these things to help you with the set-up. At Social Star we help our clients with this process, from selecting and buying the URL to building the website and finding a host. But if you are unable to use our services, there are other options to get help. For more information, you can always search on YouTube for how to host a website. If you are technically inclined, most major host vendors have help sections on their websites, or a phone helpline to work it through with you.

Websites are probably the most lamented of the marketing tools I come across. It's vary rare to find someone who loves their website and has used it as an effective communication and marketing tool. The issue with websites is that they can be expensive and require frequent changes. So how will your site keep up with the latest technology and changes to your business? My advice is this; don't spend a lot of time or money on your site. *Gasp!* Yes, you heard me, don't spend a lot of your money to build you a website – do it yourself! Or get someone to construct a basic one for you and update it often.

There are many good platforms for starting a website such as; WordPress, Wix, Weebly, Squarespace and so many more. Find one with templates you like, that suits your budget and is easy to use. WordPress is the most popular but you need to know a little bit of coding and to be able to troubleshoot to get the best from it. It is open-source software, which means anyone can develop templates or plug-ins for it. So if you are really into website design then this is a great one for you.

If you just want to quickly get your website up and running, you need a template platform, which allows you to easily put your content into an already designed and built website. The beauty of platforms like Squarespace, Wix and Weebly is that they are super simple to use. Of course, they lack the flexibility of WordPress, but that may suit you.

The Social Star website is in Squarespace, which is a little more complex and flexible, and at the time of writing our website designer builds all of our customer sites in there. They have great templates, email and shopping cart integration and analytics built right into the site. They make it so easy to build a site that works on the big and small screens and has everything built in so it is hard to go past them for ease of use. This is one of our main criteria for selection: we must be able to hand over a website to a client and have them easily be able to make updates and changes. We want to empower the client to manage their own brand and one important step is to be able to run their own website.

Weebly is the simplest I have found and I currently use it for my landing page for this book. It is a bit cheaper and has less functionality, so we use it for smaller one-page websites called landing pages or squeeze pages. Another platform is Wix, which sits between Squarespace and Weebly. I am sure there are more you could review and a quick Google search will show all the new players.

One of the most important parts of your website platform selection is the Content Management System or CMS. If you get someone to build your website, make sure you will have a CMS and are familiar with it before they start. It is essential that you are able to make changes to your site, such as adding blog posts and updating content, when you need to. If the back end of the website doesn't have a CMS, then you need to understand how to code to do an update, which can mean that making small changes is a nightmare and that you will be forever stuck with your website programmer to do even the smallest alterations.

I recently attended a conference on personal branding and the speaker claimed that websites were redundant and that social media is all you need. Agreed? Geez, I hope not! I actually think the opposite. While it's true your website should no longer be your sole focus, it should still be central to your business and Personal Brand. There is a degree of risk in building your brand in any one social media channel, as you have no control over what changes they make to their channel over time. They can even delete your account without notice and there is nothing you can do about it. Spreading your brand across many channels provides some safety, but I still advise people to use social media to access your market, feed them back to your home website and ask them to subscribe to your database.

Therefore, you do need a website and you should also collect email addresses and other data from your clients, which requires a database back end and email system. Most hosting providers now provide a back-end database and even e-commerce solutions as optional extras too. Think about exactly what you need in a website now and build for that, but consider your future needs as well.

My strategy is to have a personal website for my Personal Brand, a business website for each of my companies, and also landing pages, which are one-page promotional websites that you put up during a promotion and take down when you finish. That's a lot of sites, I know, but once you build them you can maintain them quite easily. Especially landing pages – they replicate what is in your business website, but are specific to one product, like a book or course you want to sell.

Google, in its Zero Moment of Truth Macro Study, says that 88 per cent of consumers research online before buying and want to see 10.4 points of information about a business before they feel ready to buy their service or product[6]. This is why my strategy is to have as many URL links as possible on page one of the organic search results section of Google when a consumer searches for my service or my name. The best situation is that they keep coming across your content when they are investigating potential service providers, in the form of websites, blogs, social media, news articles and pictures. You want to dominate your particular niche so you'll need many sites to do this. Use as many social media sites as you can manage to establish your community and Personal Brand. Then drive this community to your personal or business website, to capture their details and email them regularly with valuable content and special offers. Your website should help you make money – it is the commerce engine in your digital plan, so it's essential to maintain.

The personal websites we construct for our clients at Social Star are very simple and specific. They have the client's photo, biography, blog, social media links, contact details, contact forms and some imagery, and words that best represent their brand. Some sites contain products and shopping carts, but they are business websites and we are focusing on brand websites here. In the Understand Yourself section we created a digital diagnosis document that forms the basis for the brief we give the website designer. We use designers, not developers, as the template sites we use are already built to best practice so the work we do is really on the front end of the website, not the back end. My belief is to buy the best, not create it myself, in order to save time and money. Also, the

---

6 www.google.com.au/think/research-studies/the-zero-moment-of-truth-macro-study.html

platform creators will continue to develop the back end of the website for any new developments in technology, like a new phone platform or Google SEO change. This would normally require an upgrade of your website from a developer, but not with our sites.

Once we choose the templates, colours, fonts and layout of their site and have the content, it only takes a few days to create the website and make it live. The more care the client has taken in the *Understand* section and the more assets (such as pictures, graphics, logos and videos) they have ready, the easier it is to develop the website and move on to other important steps in the process.

Some clients find having a personal website confronting and feel that it involves too much self-promotion. I reassure them that this part of your brand is not driven by ego but by a need to inform your potential clients about what you do and who you are. After all, when constructing a Personal Business you are essential to your product or service, so clients are interested in you. They want to know your background, your 'why', and how you can help them. Don't make it difficult for customers to find you. If your client can't find you and googles your service instead, they might find a competitor and not come back. Best to be easy to find.

The best way to match you to your business is via a personal website. Nothing will rank as high for your name as your own website. Furthermore, as discussed, Google tells us that consumers look at an average of 10.4 pieces of information before making a purchase. They want to see a decent amount of content before making a decision, so you need more than just one web link for them to review. Your website is one link, then your social media are all separate links that may or may not appear depending on how unique your name is. Therefore, you need to direct your prospective customers to your social media via your personal website in case you can't get prominence with it organically. Put simply, if you have a personal website you can control where your customers go when they google you. That alone is worth the effort!

BLOGS

One useful part of any website and Personal Brand is a blog. I don't recommend blogs for everyone, as it depends on whether you can really commit to it and whether it suits your brand and audience. If a blog adds value to your platform, then there is no better way to get SEO for your website, promote your expertise and display your individuality. The downside is that it is time-consuming and it can take years to establish a regular audience. But once you have that, you know you have made it as a leader in your area.

Blogs can be defined as a platform on which an individual or group of users post opinions and information on a regular basis, often about a particular topic. They are a powerful mechanism to attract people to your business. They help position your brand, convince people of your knowledge, and reveal more of your personality to keep potential and existing customers connected to you from a business perspective. They are like a regular conversation with your audience about your values, thoughts and beliefs, which are essential ingredients in a strong Personal Brand.

Being committed to blogging regularly can be daunting, especially if you have a busy life with kids, work and social activities. Of course, you are likely to be excited and motivated in the few months after you start the blog, in which time you may write many posts, but this enthusiasm can soon dwindle. It can take years to establish your credibility and audience, so it's vital to do some careful planning at the start to help you keep motivated and regularly contributing posts.

A few things to consider when starting a blog are the focus, the regularity, the format and your audience. The first consideration is, 'What am I trying to say?' That is, what unique content do you have that would make someone subscribe to your blog and keep reading regularly? And how will it help your business and Personal Brand?

The focus of your blog needs to come from your truest self. I believe everyone has something they really want to share with the world, and your blog should start from there. Think about what you wished someone had shared with you when you were young that could have helped with your life. Feel what is inside you and bursting to get out. Think, perhaps, of the sort of conversation that you love having with a close friend when you feel like you are really helping them. This is where it starts.

Next, think about the unique knowledge, experience and expertise you have gained in your field. This should also be shared. If you're young and don't have years of experience behind you, don't be concerned. To paraphrase a famous adage: wisdom doesn't come from being old, it comes through learning from your experience.

As I've mentioned, regularity is an important part of blogging. My advice is to post regularly, but aim for a realistic frequency based on your ability to deliver. I think it's preferable to have your blog come out at a certain time each month or week, so your audience knows when to expect it, rather than to try to produce a blog every second day but then fail to deliver. Set an expectation with your audience and then meet it. My goal is to blog once a week, and I now pre-write these so I have a backup if I get distracted or am travelling, sick or busy.

The format of blogs has changed over time. As I mentioned earlier, the internet has shifted to people preferring more images and fewer words. When people are using the web, their attention spans are usually short. Therefore, it's preferable to use succinct text with structured use of headings, alongside pictures and videos, rather than long text-based content. That said, there is sometimes a need to post some detailed content to fully explore a topic. I think a combination of short, punchy posts and longer prose can work to establish your competence in an area but also keep people interested.

Blogs can be run on your website via platforms such as Blogger, TypePad and WordPress, or as a separate blog not attached to your website. If you run it on your website you get the benefit of having more words on the internet for search engines to match against people's searches, which will draw more traffic to your site. Remember that only words are picked up by search engines, so if you put pictures in your blog posts, be sure to include relevant meta tags, called alt tags – descriptive words attached to the image – to attract traffic.

YOUR LOGO

Another part of building your Personal Brand is considering a logo – something to differentiate you or your brand name from other text on your website. It could be as simple as a specific font for your name, or a small icon related to your brand. Recently at Social Star we worked with an art dealer who wanted to move his business and brand from buying and selling art to being an art advisor who was considered an expert in the field. We set about thinking of something unique that distinguished him – his 'thing', as I call it, which we will discuss in more detail later. His 'thing' was always wearing a hat and he had been doing it so long that everyone associated it with his persona and brand. So when constructing his personal website, we simply drew a hat on one letter of his logo to add something different.

A small element such as this can be really useful when completing the finishing touches to your website. As can a 'favicon', which is the small picture you see at the beginning of the URL bar at the top of a webpage. For Facebook it is an 'F' in a blue box; with Social Star it is a red star, and for my art consultant client it is his little hat logo. A designer can easily create one of these now that you know you need one!

The simplest logo for your Personal Brand is your name, so we recommend you start with this as your logo. Ensure you get it in .eps .ai and .jpg file formats so you can modify it later if you need to.

TAG LINES

Coming up with a tag line that truly represents your Personal Brand and your business is half art and half science. The line should be descriptive enough that people understand what you do, but creative enough to be specific to you. Your tag line should include some of the words that you came up with in your mood board exercises. If you haven't completed the mood boards properly, go back and do them again, as we will refer to them regularly.

The field of Personal Branding is relatively new, so when I was devising my tag line, I wanted to link my extensive experience in conventional marketing with my deep knowledge of new forms of promotion. The tag line I eventually chose was: *'Marketing expert focusing on social media and personal branding'*. The combination, I feel, is unique. It differentiates me from the millions of people who work in traditional marketing, as well as the emerging technologists flocking to new marketing. Most of my older peers do not lead the new marketing revolution – that is left to young people who grew up with social media.

While the new generation may be able to execute the 'how to' of Personal Branding, without long years of business experience, they can struggle with the 'why'. My tag line effectively sells my balance of advantages.

If you are a high-profile businessperson within a corporation, your tag line might be inspired by the role you serve. So a Chief Financial Officer may have '*Professional number-lover and creative accountant*' if they wanted to be seen as dynamic and relaxed in their senior position. Another approach for the same CFO could be to position him- or herself as a serious strategist with the line '*Senior accountant creating game-changing financial strategies for large corporations*'. It really depends on how you want to be perceived.

One of my favourite examples was our art dealer-turned-art expert who now provides '*Bespoke art advice for the discerning investor*'. He wanted to position himself as providing a tailored service to wealthy clients, hence the word 'bespoke'. But he also had to specify what it was he actually did, which is where 'art advice' came in. Finally, he wanted to spell out what type of client he wished to attract, which was large collectors, so 'discerning investors' was chosen.

A good tag line should convey several messages succinctly and snappily, and is particularly important for LinkedIn and Twitter, as you shall see later on. Your tag line will change over time as the market and your business change. Every change you make to your brand needs to filter across all of your social media and web presences and will send an update to your community, so be aware of how regularly you make changes. Once you position yourself to the market in a certain way, you will be remembered in that light – so slight adjustments to your brand are fine, but wholesale changes will require a little effort to inform your market about why you made the change. I will review brand changes later in the book, as it is an important part of the process.

THE 'THING'

The 'thing' is one defining aspect of your brand or personality trait that sets you apart from your competitors. Think of Steve Jobs, the genius of Apple computers, and imagine him in your mind for a moment. If you are picturing him in a black skivvy and blue jeans on stage holding the latest beautifully designed Apple product, there is a reason for that. He wore that same out-fit to product launches for twenty years, and consequently it is how most people remember him. Did he do it on purpose or was it that he placed little value on clothes and couldn't be bothered changing into something more formal? Who knows, but it was an effective 'thing' that he did with clothing. In Australia, the well-known restaurant critic and TV personality Matt Preston dresses in a particularly dapper style and always with a cravat. Molly Meldrum, the TV music personality, always wears a cow-boy hat. Richard Branson is known for his crazy stunts, but also for his long hair and beard. They all have their 'thing'.

Having a 'thing' isn't a mandatory part of the branding pro-cess, but it does help in standing out from the crowd. It is also based in neuro-linguistic programing, which involves examining how the brain works with regard to our senses, language and memory. If you have ever studied advanced memory techniques, you might have come across the mental-hook idea. When the brain is presented with a new piece of information, it needs a mental 'hook' to place that information on. For instance, when you meet people for the first time, how do you remember them? It could be their name, the way they look, what they do, where you meet them, what they wear or a unique part of their personality. How you remember them is determined by a combination of your values and sensory preferences.

For example, if your senses are very visually attuned and you place a high value on physical appearance, you might remember people by distinguishing physical features, such as long legs, a bald head or a big nose. Perhaps your values are more work-related and you sense things in more of a physical way. You might recall the company a person works for and how they shook your hand. This could stick in your mind as, say, the 'strong grip from Accenture' or the 'cold hand from IBM', rather than that person's name or what clothes they were wearing.

Having a 'thing' can help other people to remember you. It should be something that is natural and easy to reproduce over time. Matt Preston places a high value on fashion and personal presentation, so he doesn't need to be reminded to shop for new cravats, he literally has hundreds!

One of our first clients at Social Star had a 'thing' that was more subtle than most. She was a young and successful woman working her way up the corporate ladder and we worked closely together for a few years. She was blonde and vivacious with a figure that caught people's attention. Being beautiful with an open and outgoing personality, she was concerned that she wouldn't be taken seriously in the boardroom. Before she worked with us on her branding, she toned her look down in her profile photos. This included wearing glasses and putting her hair in a bun. She thought that looking more conservative would be better for her career.

After our branding process, we decided that her 'thing' was actually her wonderful smile and engaging energy. We represented this with carefully chosen photography based on her heroes' pictures, which she selected during the mood board part of the branding process. Reese Witherspoon was chosen as a desirable model: blonde, beautiful, smart, sassy and someone to be taken seriously. We examined photos of Witherspoon and how she positioned herself, then modelled our client on that example. She bloomed in her brand as it was a natural fit, rather than the constrictive one she had thought would be best, and she is now doing amazing things in corporate land.

To find your 'thing', I suggest thinking about what defining features a cartoonist would pick up on if they were to draw a caricature of you. Then go into Google, Facebook or your computer and scroll through photos of yourself. What 'thing' keeps reappearing all the time, regardless of the situation you're in? Is it an expression, an item of clothing, the way you act? Finally, ask your friends what stood out for them the first time you met.

Was it your handshake, your laugh, your eyes, your energy level or something else completely?

Whatever it is, when you find it, use it in your online Personal Branding so that people are aware of it and link it back to you if you meet them in person.

I have found this part of my process the most challenging. I am average height and average weight, with no really defining physical features. My name is common and my dress sense is not highly creative. So on first meeting, many people think I look vaguely familiar. People generally warm to me quickly and open up to tell me about themselves, as I love to hear their stories and when we leave they have a positive impression of me. But I need to leave them with a mental hook to remember me. It really depends on where they meet me, but usually they think of me as the 'Marketing guy' or the 'Digital guy'. Which brings me to probably the single most important part of the whole Personal Brand process: positioning.

POSITIONING

I read a book when I first started my marketing undergraduate degree called *Positioning: The Battle for Your Mind*, by Al Ries, Jack Trout and Philip Kotler. It was additional reading rather than a compulsory text, yet it had more impact on me than any other textbook I read at that time. It is a small book and you can read it in one sitting, as I did. The essence of it is that the basis of all marketing is to gain a position in the consumer's mind – based on the values you represent – ahead of your competition. All the branding, marketing and money you spend is wasted if the consumer has a different perception of you and your brand than what you are aiming for. It doesn't matter what you think your brand is – what matters is what is in the consumer's mind. Once they've committed to a perception of you, it is very difficult to change it.

Think of Volvo – do you perceive them as a sporty car maker? Probably not. Most would know them for safety, but they tried unsuccessfully for a decade to change their image to that of a sporty brand. Similarly, when an actor makes music or a musician tries to act, we judge them as being in the wrong place. Our positioning of them is fixed and it seems 'wrong' to see them doing something different. That's why changing your positioning generally doesn't work. Michael Jordan, the best basketballer of all time, playing baseball?

So, in our Personal Branding process at Social Star, we carefully set a clear and specific position for you in the market. You are locking that brand into consumers minds.

A great way to understand your position relative to those in your industry is to create a perceptual map. Draw two axes on a bit of paper: the Y axis is top to bottom and the X axis is left to right. Label these axes with your two highest traits that we used in the mood board exercise, and then draw a plus symbol in the middle of the two axes. The challenge is to plot yourself and the other people in your industry on the perceptual map relative to each other as your market would see it. If this sounds confusing, google 'perceptual maps' and you will see loads of examples.

The goal is to see where you are in the market and then to draw another circle where you would like to be. The second location is your aspirational brand position, and the purpose of following the steps in this book is to get you to that place where you are the leader in your particular industry.

Once you know how you want your brand to be perceived, it is time for one of the most important parts of your brand and the most often used: your photo.

PHOTOGRAPHY

The internet might have been written in binary code with zeros and ones, but social media is based on photos and words, so the quality of your pictures and words is paramount. I fully believe that you need to get a professional photographer to do these shots, and no, your friend who knows a bit about cameras is not good enough. It should only cost between $200 and $500 for a quality picture, which is a great investment given that you can use it for several years. It will be used on your biography, your website and all your social media channels so it will get plenty of use.

You only need one quality shot, but I usually recommend getting at least three so you can change them around and use them for different purposes. It's best to have one close-up colour headshot on a white background, shot in a studio with at least two lights. You can also try black backgrounds, but they change the tone of the shot, so get the quality white one first. For a second shoot you may try going outdoors, but the quality of these shots will vary depending on the light and weather, plus natural light will show up any flaws in your skin, and if the light is too strong it can make you squint. It's also much harder to style your clothing to match the background. For all these reasons I prefer indoor shoots – they are more reliable and your eyes will be more open. Remember, the eyes are the key.

Pose facing towards the camera with your eyes looking directly into the lens. I look at a lot of shots and I can instantly tell when someone is trying to pose. Don't do it. Relax and just be you. Think about your favourite thing to do in business. It might be being on stage speaking to hundreds of people, or being in a strategy session or meeting with clients. Inspiration is sexy, so if you feel inspired about your business then the camera will capture it. Have you ever noticed how artists or sports people look amazing and beautiful when they are on the stage or the field, but out of their element they can look awkward and plain? The difference is inspiration. If you have a good photographer who specialises in headshots, they will do the lighting and encourage you to try out many different facial expressions. Be full of life and smile widely, as your expressions always appear more subdued in the actual pictures. This is your time to shine!

Remember, this is a basic face shot to show your potential clients who you are – it needs to look just like you. So keep make-up and Photoshop retouching to a minimum. If your clients can't recognise you from your picture, you have gone too far. It isn't a fashion shoot either, so wear clothes you love and feel comfortable in. Dress as if it's for an important meeting with a perfect client. If you feel good, you will look good. Bring at least three changes of clothes, as some will work better with your facial tone and the shoot background.

For me, my preferred outfit is a suit with no tie, because that suits my brand. I use this on my LinkedIn account, Twitter and the biography of my personal website, www.andrewford. com.au. I then have a full-body secondary shot. You should have a full-body image in case it's needed for use in something such as a book cover or on an 'about me' section on your website, where you can fit a longer shot. See my about.me/fordy page for an example. The third shot I recommend getting is in casual attire, mainly for use on Facebook, but it can also be used for Pinterest, Twitter, Instagram, or any other friends-based social platform.

Make sure you get as many of the raw photos – that is, in a high-resolution JPEG format – as you can, but also get your 'hero shots' in both raw format and smaller sizes too. You will need all these varieties for different applications. For print you need high resolution, but for social media they generally set upload limitations, and the image quality doesn't need to be as high on screen, so you need a smaller size.

Why are pictures so important? If you search on Google Images or social platforms you will see a result list that has about twenty pictures and a few lines of text – that is what your potential clients will see when they are looking for you. Do you stand out? Are you represented as specifically and powerfully as you could be? This is your one opportunity to stand out and grab a person's attention, so great pictures are vital!

YOUR PROFESSIONAL BIOGRAPHY

The résumé is dead. Well, not really dead, but less important than it use to be. Now there is a suite of ways to communicate your work experience and expertise. LinkedIn is the new place for business information. As well as a Google search, the vast majority of recruiters use LinkedIn to find you, and so do customers and potential partners in your business (but more in the Social Media section on LinkedIn). So what is a good addition to your résumé? The answer: a professionally written biography.

A biography is not like a résumé. Résumés are data-driven, with dates and titles, and without any room to add the personality and texture that really tells people who you are and what you do. Biographies do contain details of relevant work history, education and achievement, but in a succinct form and designed to highlight your values and character. That's why they work well together. If you have a biography and a résumé, and both of them are on LinkedIn, you have a foundation of information to support your Personal Brand. The only extra part would be a personal video, but more on that in the section on video later.

There is an art and some science to a professional biography that doesn't just read like the bio of an average businessperson, so it is wise to seek guidance and examples to ensure that yours is authentic and powerful. You can find an example of my own bio online at www.andrewford.com.au/about or join me on LinkedIn to see how I have put it all together. A biography is a blend of what you would convey to someone through both your résumé and a face-to-face meeting. It should list your credentials, but also showcase your personality. Someone should be able to read it and get a really good sense of your values and character. Find a quality biography writer who specialises in Personal Branding and get them to write a 500-word bio for you. You should use all of this text as a ready-made press bio and for your personal website.

A smaller version, approximately three paragraphs in length, is needed for your LinkedIn profile and an even smaller version should be used for social media. As I am invited to speak at various events and to judge business-plan competitions, the first thing organisers always ask me is to send a high-resolution photo and a bio for their website and marketing materials. I delight them by sending them immediately, as they normally have to endlessly chase people for them. It shocks me that some speakers don't have these on hand; you should always be prepared with these two essential elements of your Personal Brand.

If you want to have a go at writing your own biography I have a step by step process below, however, I would urge you to get a professionally written one eventually.

To write your own bio I recommend you have five paragraphs similar to your personal pitch, which we will cover in more detail in the Leverage section. The five sections are:

1. Who you are – position your personality and why they should care.

2. What you do now – your role and the benefits of that for the reader.

3. Your credibility – what skills, education and experience you have.

4. What you want – describe the clients you are looking for.

5. Your why – a personal message about why you do what you do with a quote.

Each paragraph should be two or three sentences long, with clear points. Once you have this sample, give it to some people you respect to see if it accurately reflects you and how they perceive you. Words are the essence of SEO – maximising the visibility of your site. They are essential to making yourself easily findable online. They convey your position in the market, your value to the client and why your service should be chosen over that of a competitor. You only have a few lines to articulate your mission to your perfect client, so the words you use should be professionally written. The most important words related to your Personal Brand are your tag line and your biography. Or if this process is too hard, get a personal video!

VIDEO

There's one final element of your Personal Brand that combines both images and words: video. This is an optional element and not as necessary as photography and words alone, but is becoming more popular every day. The main benefit of video is that it is the most easily digestible form of communication for clients, aside from a face-to-face meeting. This is why television advertising is so strong, because you can communicate so much more in thirty seconds than you could in a print or radio ad for the same campaign.

To effectively use video, you need to have a good understanding of the medium and to make a more significant investment of time and money; this is why I list it as an optional extra. A personal video is basically an interview of you, where someone will ask you the five questions listed in the biography section above. You can add this to your LinkedIn profile and personal website as it makes a great addition to your content.

Another good use of video is video blogs – simply known as 'vlogs'. I recorded a bunch of these recently for a company called Take 10 Social and you can find these on YouTube. They were produced and recorded by myself, so the quality is basic, but the messages I deliver are clear and strong.

If you wish to record a video of yourself, you will need the right equipment. For my vlogs, I used a Canon 60D digital SLR camera with a high-definition video mode, a tripod, two lights and a lapel microphone. I know others who have a $300 camera especially for video. While most laptops have built-in webcams, I wouldn't recommend using one as the quality is often poor and it restricts your body position and distance from the camera. In terms of a background, I used a white wall with my degrees hung up behind me, a simple but effective touch. I also had a friend edit the videos and clean them up, for a professional polish. If you want a professional look and high quality, you can use a professional camera operator and video editor, but it all depends on what you're using the video for, your budget and the style of your Personal Brand.

My recommendation with videos is that you should upload them to the video-based social media sites and link to them on your website. So upload them onto YouTube and Vimeo (which is a professional version of YouTube), then copy the code that the site provides and put it into your website. The video will then play inside your website but you can track how many plays it's had back to YouTube.

SOCIAL MEDIA

Social Media is defined by Mirriam-Webster online dictionary as 'forms of electronic communication (as Web sites for social networking and microblogging) through which users create online communities to share information, ideas, personal messages, and other content (as videos)'[7].

---

7 www.merriam-webster.com/dictionary/social%20media

Social media relies on mobile and web-based technologies to create highly interactive platforms. Andreas Kaplan and Michael Haenlein, experts in the field, explain that it 'introduces substantial and pervasive changes to communication between organisations, communities and individuals'[8]. More simply, however, I describe social media as a dinner party on steroids.

What you get out of this following section will vary remarkably from person to person, depending on your work situation and goals. If you work in a large company you will have to adhere to corporate social media guidelines. If you are a professional running your own business you will have to consider how much time you really have to devote to learning and operating multiple digital channels. For those in a small business, you will need to consider how to run your personal channels with your business channels, who will tweet, how many Facebook pages you want to run, and what sort of blog you want. If you are in a new business start-up you will probably want to do everything! Resist the temptation to do too much; my advice to clients is to start with the essentials, which are a personal website – and business website if you have a business brand – and positioning on either Facebook or LinkedIn, depending on your brand, as well as a blog. Other mandatories include owning your physical place on Google+ and a few other tricks we will soon discuss. Once you are comfortable running your basic digital platform, you can expand your scope to include more channels.

---

8 Kaplan, Andreas M. & Haenlein, Michael (2010). 'Users of the world, unite! The challenges and opportunities of social media'. Business Horizons. 53 (1), p. 61.

Remember, marketing on digital media is a time-consuming effort, so it is important to choose your mediums carefully, as when you start it is hard to stop doing it. I also want to reinforce the difference between social media and your own websites. With social media, you don't own the platform. The content and database attached to free mediums such as Facebook or LinkedIn are not under your control. In fact, they own any asset you put on there. They can change the rules at any time, and if you read the terms and conditions carefully, you will see that they can also do things with your content – the most basic being to share your data with advertisers so they can target you. Privacy laws mean they will not provide your specific details, but they could use your data in ways you haven't considered.

The real risk, however, is that you can invest enormous amounts of time and, potentially, money in setting up your social media accounts and the layout and set-up can be significantly altered, or worse, your entire account can be taken down. When Facebook went to Timeline, I knew many clients who had invested considerable time and money to develop their Facebook pages with custom applications and design, only to have to completely redo it when Timeline was forcibly introduced. I have also seen clients' Twitter accounts taken down when they grew 'too fast', however, they were all restored in a few days.

The only platform you can rely on is the one you own and build, and that's your website. Then you have a dedicated hosting provider and a platform under your control. Your database is relatively safe from changes and you at least have the ability to back up your content. The main issue then is security, and it is imperative you maintain it on your site so it doesn't get hacked.

With that warning out of the way, I will say that social media is the single biggest access point you have for engagement with new clients. It is not an effective sales tool just yet, but it's slowly but surely heading that way. Its purpose is to have clients find you, engage with your brand and head to your website to make a purchase. I'll go through each social media platform separately, starting with the biggest and most well known: Facebook.

Facebook

Facebook was launched in February 2004, created in Mark Zuckerberg's college dorm room. If you have seen the movie *The Social Network*, you know the story. I clearly remember the first time I saw Facebook. I was working for the software division of Hewlett-Packard in Melbourne. A friend called me over to see this new site that was hot in California and it looked pretty unimpressive, with bland graphics and an un-customisable layout. So I ignored it and moved on to MySpace, which was so cool at the time! All these years later, MySpace has well and truly lost its market share, while Facebook is the most powerful social network in the world with more than a billion users and counting. There are a few Chinese sites that will approach that figure soon, due to the sheer size of that country's population, but as these sites only operate in China, where Facebook isn't available, I will leave these out of my recommendations. Facebook is as powerful as Google in terms of advertising but they will battle for your advertising dollar until the next big site arrives.

What is so compelling about Facebook is not just its sheer number of members, but the quantity of information they have on each person. On my Facebook sites, there are hundreds of photos, status updates, 'likes' on others' pages, comments, as well as the dozen or so business pages I manage. Facebook owns all of this content! Yes, they own your photos and can use these if they choose, so be careful with what you give them. A quick tip if you want to check what's in your Facebook: you can download a copy of your history, which includes all the stuff you have deleted, as they keep everything.

There are two main ways to leverage Facebook for your business benefit. One is to create a Personal Brand via a personal profile, and the other is with a business page. Let's start with personal pages, which are designed for individuals to interact with friends. For someone to see your content they send you a 'friend request' and you can accept or decline them to be part of your community. The amount of information strangers and your own friends can see depends on the privacy settings you choose, and you have quite a bit of flexibility in how you share your profile. When you post something on your personal page, your friends will see it in their news stream.

That said, Facebook is now restricting how much content your friends see, based on an algorithm that analyses who you interact with and who interacts with you. If you always go and look at a certain friend's page and 'like' their content, their content will appear in your stream. But if you haven't interacted with a friend for a long time, their content will disappear from your feed, and vice versa. The reason Facebook made this change was to ensure that you are only getting relevant content, but also so that if you want to get a post to all of your friends, you have to pay for it. At the time of writing, an average post will reach less than thirty per cent of your friends, but Facebook will push it to all of your friends for a variable fee. Remember, the site isn't a free public service – it's a commercial business listed on the stock exchange with investors wanting a return on their money, so expect more of these revenue-generating schemes to pop up in the future. My prediction is that Facebook will keep looking for ways to charge users until the site resembles a sort of bank, where if you want to interact with someone or do anything there will be a fee.

The other way to use Facebook is to create a page allowing fans of an individual, business, product, service, charity and so on, to 'like' or subscribe to the page. Pages look much like a user's private personal profile, but they are integrated with Facebook's advertising system. You don't have to approve 'likes' on your page, so anyone who 'likes' it will instantly be able to see your content.

There are pages for most things you can imagine, and it is easy to see the different types when you set one up to suit your particular situation. Most of my clients are either celebrities who use a fan page or businesses who create a business page. The benefit of a business page is that you can form it around a person, an organisation, charity, company, or whatever you want. Unlike a personal profile, which has its friend limit capped at 5000, there are no restrictions on the number of people who can join your community.

My clients always ask me whether a private profile or a public page is best and the right answer really does depend on your situation. I generally recommend the following strategy: there are friend/friend, friend/business and business/business pages. A friend/friend profile is your personal profile, which you need to set up any other pages or groups. If you want to make it private for your close friends, just adjust the privacy settings so that Google can't see it and you have to be a friend to access content. Then make a friend/business profile for your work friends, boss or staff, customers and others that you want to communicate with but you don't want them to see everything you do. The business/business pages are purely about work and are the only ones you don't have to directly manage yourself; you can get staff or agencies to do this as it isn't your primary voice. Of course, the level of authenticity in the tone of voice depends on how personal your brand is. Some people, such as Oprah, share their whole lives online, whereas others such as Richard Branson only share business-oriented information. I suggest to clients to rate their level of personalisation out of 10 and then share that with their brand managers. In the end, how you use Facebook depends on your personality, how your audience interacts with you and how big your brand is.

One local Australian celebrity that I was advising had a great opportunity on a popular TV show to gain more traction with his brand. I advised him to change his personal Facebook profile to a fan page as he was approaching the maximum number of friends. Unfortunately he was busy and didn't follow the advice, and so when he maxed out on his friends he missed the opportunity to connect with more of his fans. When he launched his fashion range, this extra reach would have been beneficial. Furthermore, those 5000 fans could see *all* of his past personal posts and photos. In a fan page they cannot see your personal page details so there is much better control of the content.

Another reason why public pages for business are so popular is that unlike Twitter, if your fans notice a post in their stream, they can see all of the content upfront without having to click a link to an external website. In my opinion, this makes it much easier for things to 'go viral' on Facebook than on Twitter. Also, as Facebook is the biggest social network, there is more of a chance that potential clients will see you interacting with other profiles and pages, thereby increasing your exposure. This is great if you are trying to make a name for yourself and your brand.

You can also create numerous pages and groups to segment your community and have private discussions with them. This is a great way to make your brand more exclusive and encourage more open dialogue, as these can be made private. I have several pages for different businesses and personal interests, plus groups for my friends, alumni and other communities where we don't want to share information publicly. One of the nice features of groups and pages is that you don't have to be friends with someone to have them in your group, so it keeps your other profile separate. There are too many features to discuss them all here, but suffice to say, get on Facebook and start working it!

Facebook, unlike Twitter, allows for social analytics, so you can actually see the number of people who are interacting with your brand. This is extremely important for determining a return on investment (ROI) for your time and effort. Facebook also brings out new features all the time so to keep up to date on this site, subscribe to a well-known blog for updates.

Another way to leverage Facebook is to advertise on it. Think about all the information people put on this site – so much of their lives is on display. You can use this information to target advertising to just about any parameter, including geographic location, gender, marital status, education, job title, birthdate and family size, and interests such as books, music, products and recreational activities, brands, people and much more! Essentially, if you have 'liked' a page, then I can target an ad to you based on that 'like'. So on my private Facebook I 'like' Porsche cars; this means that Porsche could advertise to me if I meet their demographic profile based on my age, education, job and family status and they decide to target an ad to me.

Advertising on Facebook is super easy to do, is very cost effective and it works. There is a vast array of advertising options on Facebook and the simplest are getting people to 'like' your page or getting people from Facebook to your external web-site. In my opinion, it's more efficient to use Facebook ads to get people to your page, where they can see your content and decide if they like what you have, and then go to your website if they are interested. Otherwise you're paying a lot of money for people to go to your website, only to bounce right off it. Another method that has become quite popular is targeting the fans of related pages. This allows you to send promotional messages to people who 'like' pages similar to yours. Ads on Facebook are useful to start the ball rolling on your brand but if you have to pay for traffic long term, then your brand really isn't working for you. The whole premise of a strong Personal Brand is that it attracts people to it.

Facebook, like any social media site, should be used to attract potential customers with interesting and engaging content and then communicate with them, while your website is for selling things and making money. You need to make friends with your community and demonstrate your value in the 'safe' social media environment before you try to push them to your website.

A tip about branding on Facebook is to always get a designer to make your background picture. There are some restrictions on what you can put in the image, such as advertising messages and URLs, so use that space as a positioning tool. You have a huge space to present your brand essence, so take that one optimal trait we worked on in the Understand section and get an image that best represents you.

The bottom line about Facebook is you need to be on it, regardless of whether you are going to use it as a primary channel or not. It is too big to ignore and it is a great place to build your community and attract consumers to your website. As I've said, the best strategy is to use attraction sites like Facebook to bring people to your website, rather than using social media platforms as your primary sites.

LinkedIn

LinkedIn is the quiet achiever of the social media space. It has solidly grown its membership to over 250 million users and has an extremely high-quality database for certain types of marketing. Where Facebook is your social home, LinkedIn is your business home. I don't even have a résumé anymore, as I can simply keep my LinkedIn profile updated and push the PDF button and hey presto, there's my résumé to email or print. Sure, it isn't as detailed as a résumé should be and for some professions such as academia or medical professions a résumé is vital. But as a digital marketer, not having a résumé hasn't stopped recruiters calling me and businesses offering me work.

Having a solid LinkedIn profile is an absolute must. If you're not on LinkedIn, create your profile now and as we run through the book you can add the essential elements to make it more robust. LinkedIn, like Facebook, is a connection site. You need to request a connection to a person and if they accept then you can see their information and contacts. It is a daisy chain where you connect with people and then their contacts, and then their contacts' connections, and so on. Information on LinkedIn is not based on pictures, pithy comments and 'likes'. In fact, in the past you couldn't upload a picture to LinkedIn apart from your profile shot! Now you can use PDF, PowerPoint, videos and pictures, basically any file you want to share as part of your profile. You can post comments in the update stream, which your connections will see, and you can link to websites, so essentially it's the same content as what's on Facebook, just with a different tone of voice.

The site is commercial in nature, so it is safe to présumé that people will only connect with you to talk business. There are business pages and working groups all dedicated to certain topics, but be careful with groups as they are for sharing information, not selling. If you want to sell something, contact a person directly rather than posting a sales message. Understanding the cultural etiquette of social media sites is important, but when you start to use them you will quickly get to know the language and socially acceptable ways to work.

The groups on LinkedIn are not as active as those on Facebook from my experience, and don't have as many cool features such as creating events. That said, it really depends on your strategy so consult your brand manager to check which areas you should focus your time and energy on. Time is finite and social media isn't, so be careful with your most precious resource!

In my professional situation, I use Facebook and LinkedIn equally. Facebook is for my business, entrepreneurial and university connections – of course, there's a social aspect, but I post work-related content if I think it will add value to my community. LinkedIn is for my corporate friends and contacts. I don't follow the status updates as regularly as I do on Facebook, but that said, when I have a particular use for LinkedIn, having their database there is very useful.

As with Facebook, there is a distinction between a personal and a business page on LinkedIn. You need a personal LinkedIn page to create a company page. If you have a company, then I would definitely create a company page where you can upload your products and basic details. LinkedIn doesn't require the volume of updates that Facebook does as it is less a two-way communication vehicle and more like a website facility. This is a great benefit of LinkedIn, as you can create a personal profile and a company page and let it be found in Google, so you have greater SEO and access to the millions of LinkedIn users. Be sure to tailor your settings so you are notified via email if someone contacts you, in case it takes you a while to notice it in LinkedIn. You should review your site a few times a week and add connections regularly, but if you have limited time you can essentially set up your LinkedIn profile and let it sit there working for you.

One key difference in the way LinkedIn works from Facebook is that you can pay for premium access. The site revolves around information: you want to see and find people who may be in your target market, or a key supplier, so you need to find out more about them before making contact. LinkedIn will let you see primary and secondary connections, so if you have a contact, you can see their résumé and those of their friends, and can send them a message. But you aren't able to message or see the details of third-level connections who are outside your contacts and your connections' contacts, unless you pay to upgrade your profile to a premium level. There are currently three premium levels and the one you choose depends on your industry and strategy.

The other side of LinkedIn is advertising. You can target all the parameters that are in a LinkedIn profile via ads; however, the set-up, reporting and effectiveness of LinkedIn ads are not as good as with Facebook. In fact, you may be surprised to learn that money from ads makes up only twenty per cent of LinkedIn's total revenue. Corporate services, such as premium profiles, account for another twenty per cent, and a whopping sixty per cent comes from recruitment services. Profit drives behaviour in companies, which is why Facebook will continue to sell your content to advertisers chasing their revenue and why LinkedIn will continue to want to know about your career, so recruiters and other companies can offer you jobs.

My advice would be to avoid LinkedIn ads at this time unless you are in a field specifically related to LinkedIn. The best way to use LinkedIn is to have a great profile, connect with relevant people and form a community to push to your website when the time is right. A great way to do this is to ask your satisfied clients for a recommendation and then to store it on your profile against the relevant job role. If a happy client sent you an email to say thank you for your great work, it can be lost as a marketing tool, so thank them and see if they would you write a recommendation. Even in Facebook it would soon disappear in the volume of content down on your timeline. But in LinkedIn it is always presented when people review your profile.

I have learnt many tips and tricks on how to best use LinkedIn to connect with the perfect clients and how to construct a brilliant profile, so stay tuned to my blog to get regular updates on LinkedIn.

Twitter

Ahh, Twitter, my friend and foe! I have a love–hate relationship with this fickle site because it can be so useful and powerful but is a hard nut to crack. On Facebook and LinkedIn it is possible to see steady results through diligent work, but Twitter is more random. Twitter has been described as the only medium that can communicate to the world instantly, freely and easily. No wonder emergency services are using it for natural disaster updates.

Twitter allows you to post messages – 'tweets' – to your followers, in a similar way to the status update function of Facebook. And that, more or less, is all they do – but they do it really well. It is super simple to use and I recommend that all my clients set up an account, but take note of my advice before they tweet. You connect to people or 'follow' them to form your community, the same as on Facebook and LinkedIn, however, people don't have to approve your connection, you just con-nect. Effectively, there is no barrier to the number of people you can follow or who can follow you (with some provisos). Justin Bieber has the most Twitter followers right now, with more than forty million. The people you choose to follow become part of your community and their tweets become part of your news feed, just like in Facebook. Of course, when your community grows – mine is over 100 000 – you can't easily follow the huge volume of posts. Twitter currently doesn't restrict what tweets you receive, so you create lists in order to read the content of the people you really want to follow.

Because of the mass of content on Twitter, it has also become a powerful search engine, with Twitter members con-ducting an average of four searches per day on the site[9]. This makes Twitter a great place to start mining data and connecting

9 www.statisticbrain.com/twitter-statistics/

with your customers because, unlike Facebook and LinkedIn, it is a 100 per cent open social media network. You can use online tools to search for likeminded people or users who are talking about how may resonate with your business.

The key to understanding Twitter is to think of it as being like a billboard: you can't stop people looking at it and most people who see you will not be interested in your product or service, but you hope that by broadcasting your message widely, you will find your target audience and get them engaged enough to follow you to Facebook, LinkedIn and, ultimately, your website. When I tweet to my followers, I generally get up to a dozen re-tweets (which describes when people repost your tweet to their followers), messages (when people comment on your tweet) and 'favourites' (when people add your tweet to a list of their favourite tweets). This is not a high percentage from 100 000 followers; however, the power of Twitter is the viral nature in which content can spread. When one of my followers re-tweets to their, say, 10 000 followers, several of them may also re-tweet to their followers and so on. A compelling message can circle the world in a surprisingly short amount of time. And with all the world's media and news channels following Twitter, and looking closely at 'trending' (popular) topics, it is a truly global form of communication.

There are a few basics you need to know before you use Twitter. When you want to reference a person you use the @ symbol before their username. So to reference me, write @SirFord and I will receive this message. This message won't be private though, so remember that everyone can read it!

To reference a topic, use the # symbol. An example could be: 'Welcome @SirFord to the discussion on #socialmedia'. You only have 140 characters, including spaces, to convey your message, and this includes any URL you choose to include. While you can't post a picture directly on your feed, you can post a URL link to one. Another tip is that when including a URL, shorten it with short URL like tinyurl.com, to save on characters.

If you are re-tweeted, you will get a notification, so you will know pretty quickly if your content is resonating with your target audience. Another great way of getting feedback is seeing who has 'favourited' your message. You can control your Twitter settings to regulate how many email notifications – if any – they send you when people interact with you. I have a lot of traffic on my Twitter page and manage several accounts for high-profile people, so I limit my notifications so that I only receive them when someone sends me a direct message or re-tweets one of my messages. I see who my new followers are when I log into the website.

At Social Star we use several strategies to help our clients increase their following and influence on Twitter. All of these are important and should be executed concurrently to drive the best results. The first of these strategies is to follow people with common interests to those of your brand. In our experience, if you follow a number of people who are in a related field to yours, or there is a relationship between what you do and what they are interested in, there is a fifty per cent chance these people will follow you back. So get to work, as this is a sure-fire way to quickly boost your following.

Twitter's follower thresholds restrict any user from following a certain percentage of people more than the total number of followers they have. This restricts accounts from indiscriminately following thousands of people and helps minimise 'bot' accounts (accounts that are not real people, but set up by machines) that fill up the network with spam. If you are following people as a strategy to get more followers – remembering the likely fifty per cent follow-back rate – there will be quite a number of people who won't follow you back. You need to clear these people from your following list so you are able to follow different people and continue to expand your community.

Bill Gates wrote an article in 1996 named *Content is King*[10]. This maxim should be applied when you enact your social media strategy. While the technique of following and un-following is effective in quickly building a community, you need a strong message to keep people engaged and sharing your tweets. A true follower is somebody who is actively engaged with you and is actually interested in you and/or your products.

An important rule with Twitter is to follow back people who follow you. It is common courtesy and when people use free online tools to see who isn't following them back and notice that you are one of these people, they may delete you from their follower list.

For the Social Star Twitter account, we have set up an automatic response to people who have just followed us. An

---

10 www.craigbailey.net/content-is-king-by-bill-gates/

auto-response is a great way to start a conversation when you have a large number of followers, and when you are using the follow and un-follow strategy. Another purpose of auto-responses is that after your introduction, you can push people to various other social channels to increase your following on those, or even push people to your website.

To hone your content strategy for a social media site, you need to consider the following points:

1. What is the purpose of my communication?
2. How do I add value for my fans and followers?

These two points really do go hand in hand. Put simply, one of the major reasons for your communication through social media should be to provide value to the people who are listening to you. Of course, there are always other business objectives that need to be satisfied, such as money, reach, brand awareness, promotion of brand message and mining for new clients. There are many more reasons, but those listed are the key concerns, and should be front of mind when you communicate, to ensure that you get something in return for your efforts.

How often someone should tweet is a topic that frequently comes up with our clients. People want to be able to push their messages out as regularly as possible without the risk of their brand being seen as inappropriate or spammy. The number of posts on Twitter per day with which we have seen the most success is three. Any more, and you risk repelling followers. However, you don't have to publish that regularly, as most

Twitter people just sit there and listen, it is the few who produce the most content.

If you use the methods above to grow your following on Twitter, you will quickly find yourself with hundreds of new followers. Twitter can expand your reach to new customers, but what about the people that you want to listen to? We recommend to all of our clients to use lists. You may have 30 000 followers and be following the same amount of people, but with those kinds of numbers, there is no way you will be able to keep up with your favourite people and what they are talking about. Lists can be public or private, but if you add a client to a private list they won't know that you have done so. Therefore, we tell our clients to create lists with cryptic names that only they know and then to sort their contacts into these. This way, if you have a list for your key clients, they will be able to see you have listed them, but they won't be able to understand what tier of client you have deemed them.

There is a lot to learn about Facebook, LinkedIn and Twitter! However, they are the most important social media sites, so it's essential to know how they differ and how you can make the most of them. If you use these three well, in conjunction with your website and blog, you can have great success with your Personal Brand. The other sites I'll discuss, apart from the next one, are all niche, but still worth exploring.

Google+

Google Plus is now a must-have site, not necessarily to connect to your community, but more for SEO purposes. Google is the largest internet search provider in the world and is favouring their content in search results. If you google a particular product or service you will find that Google is providing Google+ results before other organic links. If the service has a geographic location they are also giving huge prominence to the Google Places information on the top right hand of the screen. Our strategy for new clients is to include a Google+ strategy as well as LinkedIn and Facebook. To make managing this site easy, we replicate their updates from LinkedIn and Facebook onto Google+.

YouTube

YouTube quickly became the video-sharing site of choice after its launch in 2005. It was purchased by Google in 2006 for US$1.65 billion[11] and is the second-largest search engine in the world, after Google. No wonder they snapped it up – if you can't beat them, buy them, I say.

YouTube does one thing really well: it imports and saves videos and allows for them to be easily shared. It is free to upload a video and just requires a Google account to get started. Once you upload your video it can be seen on YouTube directly and is searchable through Google and other search engines; plus you can use the code provided by YouTube to display the video on your own website, which is great!

I generally recommend that clients upload their video content to YouTube first, then import the video to their websites or blogs, rather than uploading the video directly to their websites.

---

[11] www.nbcnews.com/id/15196982/ns/business-us_business/t/google-buys-youtube-billion/

There are two benefits of this. First, you get the SEO from Google and YouTube, plus you don't have to pay for the storage to host the video. Furthermore, YouTube will always invest in their video -playing technology as that is their core business, so it will keep up to date with current trends in mobile and computer software. If you load a video onto your site directly, you need to have a video player installed in order for it to play, and then it is up to you to regularly update the technology. Outsource the updates, I say!

There are other video sites, the main one being Vimeo, which is more for professional video people who want higher quality and more control over their content. Vimeo isn't a popular consumer channel, so if you want people to see your video via a Google search, YouTube is much better. But if all you are interested in is putting the video on your website, Vimeo is a good option.

Video is becoming a much more important part of marketing strategies as people's attention spans reduce. There is so much content available now that people want the most digestible format available, and video can communicate way more than words in less time. Therefore, many people are using video on their websites and emails to more efficiently communicate their messages.

Video is even taking over the blog as a more effective way of communicating with communities and attracting new followers, as discussed. In response to this, YouTube has made some great new tools to help you create, edit and post your blog directly from their site. More free tools! Due to the quality of newer smartphones, it is even possible to record from this device, but it's not necessarily recommended because the quality may still not be high enough.

Pinterest

Pinterest is one of my personal favourites and, in my opinion, will be a massive driver of traffic to websites in the future.

It is the fastest-growing social media site ever, which is kind of remarkable seeing it is, in essence, a picture-sharing site not dissimilar to Flickr and many others. The key difference with Pinterest is that it has been built with one main purpose in mind: to drive traffic to your website and generate revenue for you! It is also elegantly designed and very simple to use. I advise my clients to sign up for a free account and check it out. Whether you use it or not, it is good to watch this one as it will be big.

How it works is that you create a virtual pin board to put all the pictures you want to keep, like you would with a real pin board or scrapbook. Then you upload images from websites, your own files or images from other people's pin boards, to your own. You can search for content by pin, person or board. Pinterest is an open platform like Twitter, where you can follow anyone's board and see anyone's pins (unless they make it private), and they can do the same. That is why it is more powerful than Facebook or Flickr as a photo-sharing site. It is very popular with women in the USA, with eighty-three per cent of users being female[12]. So if you're targeting females, this site is for you!

---

12 http://econsultancy.com/au/blog/9021-more-male-pinterest-users-in-uk-than-female-infographic

However, each country is different so review the particular statistics for your target audience before embarking on a Pinterest campaign.

The business model is that users upload pictures – and sometimes videos – by copying it from either a website that retains all the URL details, or from their computer, and entering the URL where the picture comes from. The URL details are critical. When a user does a search (which is essentially a copy of a Google image search) and finds what they are looking for, they can copy the image to their board and also click on the image to go to the website to buy the item, if the image is of a product. Due to the visual nature of the site it lends itself to fashion, food and home industries, but is not limited to anything, really. On my account, I have posted images of books I love, entrepreneurs I find inspiring and info-graphics of interesting social media strategies – not all of which were based on photographs.

Even though this is a business-oriented site for users, it isn't a marketing platform like LinkedIn, and only quality content for users should be uploaded, to keep your community strong. Pure marketing messages will not be well received and will probably not result in increased traffic to your sites. Try to add value for the target audience you are trying to reach and if they like your free content, they may be tempted to share it with their followers on other social media or even click though to your website.

I believe that Facebook's popularity has plateaued, and the statistics back this up. Pinterest is gaining massive traction by doing what Facebook does with its picture-sharing function, but better. This situation is similar to department stores that used to dominate shopping because they had everything, but that are now suffering the death of a thousand cuts from all the smaller players that consumers can find online. Increasingly, quality digital niche players are leapfrogging the behemoths, and it's inevitable that the large players of today will become the shipwrecks of tomorrow.

Wikipedia

Wikipedia is another site that can be useful for your Personal Brand, and I'll include it among this list even though it isn't actually a social media site. It is purely an informational site for facts rather than self-expression. Wikipedia is essentially an online encyclopaedia, having usurped *Britannica Encyclopaedia*, which was the printed market leader for well over fifty years until digital technology made printed books less compelling. Of course, publishers of physical encyclopaedias originally resisted the change, hoping it was all a bad dream and would go away. What went away was their book sales, and now printed encyclopaedias are collectors' pieces!

The main difference between the two is that Wikipedia's content is provided by the public and Britannica was written by experts in the field. Therefore, you would expect people not to trust Wikipedia's content as much as a textbook or other reference material, but to think that is to not understand the nature of information in the new digital age. Gone are the days when information was created, held and managed by few and distributed to the many, such as with TV, radio and print media. Today everyone is both a creator and consumer of content. So people do trust the content, and when I was a teaching in the Masters of Marketing program at Swinburne University, students would reference Wikipedia constantly. It was initially rejected as a source, but due to the increased reliance that students had on this source, it gradually became acceptable, albeit frowned upon.

A key reason why Wikipedia is so popular is that there has been a cultural turnaround in the perception of authority. This relates back to the shift from a few controlling information distribution to it now being controlled by many, which I mentioned before. Now consumers have access to multiple forms of communication regarding news – Twitter, online publications, blogs and so forth – and they realise that the media isn't as impartial and factual as they perhaps thought. They don't trust the media or advertising like they used to five or ten years ago.

Wikipedia dominates search results for factual information and is the largest reference site in the world. This site gets fantastic ranking results in search engines because of the quality of the content and how frequently people are searching on it. But beware, it isn't supposed to be used for marketing or self-promotion, although it can be leveraged. It is free to use and when you have an account you can upload pages, modify content and reinforce content you agree with. All content is moderated by volunteers, and as you have to learn a new programming language to be able to upload any content, it is not for the beginner. I have created a few Wikipedia sites for clients with a high-enough profile to have a page to represent them, and it was quite challenging to get the content written in a way that was not propaganda for the person, but an unbiased account of their lives.

This site can be very useful if you have some niche and deep experience in a certain topic as it will give you more presence on search engines and help position you as an expert.

Instagram

Instagram began as a better way to take photos and post them on Facebook, but has grown into a cultish social media site for the cool kids and early adopters. Of course, Facebook noticed all the traffic being driven to their site from Instagram and promptly bought them before they could become rivals. Consequently, the pair of twenty-something Instagram founders became overnight billionaires for the eighteen months they put into developing the site[13]. Not bad work if you can get it!

The core purpose of Instagram is to make your photos look better before posting on social media sites – their stated mission is 'Fast, beautiful photo sharing'. This site is now in transformation from being one for taking, artistically editing and sharing photos, to a full-blown social platform with user profiles; but, of course, to complement Facebook, not compete with it.

Other Platforms

There are many other sites that I could review for you; however, what I've talked about are the core sites that you will come

---

13 www.smh.com.au/technology/technology-news/1b-deal-facebook-buys-instagram-mobile-photo-sharing-app-20120410-1wllb.html across and use for business. For a full review of more sites, please join my blog.

Now that you know which platforms will suit your situation, my advice is to start small. Choose only the most important ones first and build them. If you have time for more, you can add them and repurpose the content you've already created. I recommend a website, Facebook and LinkedIn to all clients. If you have a blog, you can reuse this content on Facebook or LinkedIn in a reduced word count. If you have more channels you can add pictures and use these for Instagram, Pinterest or Twitter. It all depends on the style of what you produce and your message. With that in mind, the next section on how to leverage your profile will review your voice – that is, what you are trying to say – as this is a vital last step.

CHAPTER 7

Leveraging Your Brand

'I've learned that people will forget what you said, people will forget what you did, but people will never forget how you made them feel.'
Maya Angelou

Now that you have built your platform for your Personal Brand, what are you going to do with it? It is time to find your voice – what you want to say. The message you offer usually comes from a combination of your strengths and experience. I have studied and worked in marketing for many years, so it is natural for me to communicate my thoughts about this area through my Personal Brand.

You should make the most of your strengths to enhance your brand. For instance, I channel my strengths in making presentations into creating video blogs and 'webinars'. I also use my skills in writing and networking to share my experience with new people and then use the encounters as content for social media. I take photos in our meetings and post them online as content.

YOUR CONTENT DOESN'T HAVE TO BE UNIQUE

Start with areas you are comfortable with and gradually expand your reach of topics as you go. While it is important to build on your experience, don't worry if you think that your content isn't unique. Even though you may not be creating something completely new each day, the fact that you are presenting the information means, in one sense, it is new, because no one can say it exactly as you do. Add your opinions and personality to the content to ensure it matches your brand and people will gravitate to it. Sometimes clients come to me after seeing other consultants or doing other courses because I have a fresh way of explaining the concepts they've heard but haven't understood. They finally 'get' it due to the way I communicate, and not necessarily because of the content itself.

BALANCING PROMOTION AND CONTENT

Having a strong Personal Brand is a careful balance between the promotion of your thoughts and the development of your message. Success will come when you can master both areas. If you spend all day posting on social media and building your networks, but don't convey any meaningful information, then you will seem shallow. If you spend a great deal of time creating amazing new thoughts on your focus topic, but don't share it with anyone, you will lose your opportunity to help people and capitalise on your intellectual property.

I recommend spending more time on the content creation than on promotion – you should always leave your audience wanting a little bit more. People's natural reaction to someone pushing them is to pull away. Ensure that you offer your public access to your unique content, but don't give them everything all at once. Leave some details to their imagination and allow them to step forward towards you to seek more. Doing so will cement a solid foundation of curiosity among your community and ensure the longevity of your brand. Not to mention give you opportunities to sell products!

DEFINING YOUR MARKET

The next key step is to define what you sell and who your primary and secondary markets are. This may be easy to do, or it may be complicated by the fact that you are connected with several markets.

I have a client currently who is a former professional sports-person and works in TV as a commentator, so has a solid brand in that market. However, he also has a fashion brand, a building supplies business and a marketing agency! These all involve very different markets, to say the least, so how do we stretch his brand to suit his varying client base? The answer is that he uses the same Personal Brand across all these industries. We create his brand around him and his personality, and central to this is using his sporting history and leveraging that in all his businesses, as it is his foundation brand in people's minds. Then we introduce his various companies to his audience gradually, thereby stretching his brand from that of a sporting personality to that of an entrepreneur and businessperson. His specific businesses still remain independent from a digital perspective, but over time we inject more of his Personal Brand into each to gradually connect them in consumers' minds.

That client's foundation market is sport and his secondary markets are fashion, construction and marketing. My foundation market is marketing, with a specialisation in social media and Personal Branding. What is your foundation market? To define it, think of exactly what you do and what makes you different from your competitors. The size of your market niche will depend on how you operate your business. The niche you strive to occupy needs to be large enough to fulfil your cash requirements, but small enough to be specific. In marketing this is called segmentation – one of the essential building blocks of a robust marketing plan.

It's important not to limit your perception of your market. For instance, if you have a physical service, you might think you are restricted by geography. However, in the digital age, there are other ways of doing business. Skype and email have opened up consultants to the world. You can connect with people across the globe to provide digital content and dispense your expertise. Technology allows you to expand your reach and add to your cash flow.

My business is based in consulting, which is generally face-to-face. However, I have clients who find me via referrals all across the world, and I provide my service to them via Skype and email. I don't need to live in the same city as somebody to help them set up a Personal Brand or carry out digital marketing. In fact, I have one American client who I have helped with social media whose offices are in South Africa – my business truly is a global enterprise!

You may think that going global doesn't apply to you, but keep an open mind. I have a client who is a physiotherapist, which you'd generally consider a face-to-face business. However, this client is now producing digital content to educate colleagues and is selling it online.

It is good practice to write down what your market is and then to try to size it based on your different services. Think of what you need to run your business and to be successful, then decide how broadly you need to expand your market to achieve your goals.

Another client of mine who is an architect only requires four primary customers a year! His brand is very specific and he is really only searching locally for these clients, as he doesn't need any more, but it isn't stopping him thinking globally by devising digital products to service secondary clients so that he can share his passion and bring in additional income.

Once you have defined your primary and secondary markets, and sized them appropriately, it is time to understand them in more depth.

UNDERSTANDING YOUR AUDIENCE

To more thoroughly understand your audience, you need to consider your business and how digitally savvy your consumers are. To do this, you should find current leaders in your industry and see how much digital presence they have. Which mediums do you notice being most used in your market? From my experience, the corporate market uses LinkedIn the most, entrepreneurs and smaller businesses use Facebook, fashion and the arts use Pinterest and celebrities use Twitter. For your own business, fish where the fish are. Don't expect your market to follow you to mediums that aren't suited to your industry.

There are some powerful free tools available to research where your audience is. The first is Google, which offers a treasure trove of goodies. Google is much more than a search engine – they provide so many fantastic tools. It's very worthwhile to explore their site in more detail to see what they can offer you.

Google Trends is a great resource, which displays the search volume for particular words over time, and further breaks it down by geography. For instance, if you want to search for 'Personal Branding' to see if this market is expanding globally, you just type that in and press the search button. Then you can explore each country you want to work in, to see how it compares to the global trend. (Google Trends also links to online articles related to your search term, which is a handy service.)

When you look specifically at Australia, you can see the search trends there. As you will notice from the difference between the global and Australian results, the worldwide searches for Personal Branding are much greater in volume and increasing steadily. Therefore, you could assume that the trend for this service is growing over time and will increase in Australia too, given the general lag in trends hitting Australia.

Another similar and really useful tool is Google AdWords. This tool allows you to tailor your advertising on Google so it displays when people search for particular words. The ads you see on Google at the top and side of a search page are booked using this tool. But it can be used for research too.

Once you have viewed the potential in your market, you can see how much it would cost to advertise. Google AdWords, or any search engine marketing, is one part of attraction marketing that I fully support, because it is driven by the consumer interest. The customer has a need and is searching for a solution, and at the same time you are displaying your service or product via search engine marketing.

Where many businesses fall down with digital campaigns is that once they get a potential client to their site, they don't have quality information to persuade the consumer to make the next step and contact the business. The content is either not congruent with the customer need or the information is not explicit enough about how the business can fulfil the need.

This is why at Social Star we go through the extensive process of finding out what products or services you best provide and most love to do, and then define your perfect client. When you get to the point of paying money to Google for each click they bring to you, you want to ensure that there's a high probability the client will buy what you are offering.

Via your research and with the help of the above tools, you should now understand the market you are in and how many customers you need. The next step is to specifically define who your perfect customer is.

THE ONE PERFECT CLIENT

One of the reasons we focus on understanding yourself in such detail is so that you can attract your perfect clients. As discussed, there is no use attracting customers who you don't really want to work with, or who don't suit your values or the way you prefer to work. The closer a client is to a perfect match for the product or service you provide and the way you like to provide it, the greater their satisfaction will be and the more they will promote you via word of mouth, which is the best advertising you can ever get. They will be happy to pay your fees and will be likely to hire you again.

Conversely, the further away a client is from your values and means of working, the harder it will be to please them. They are likely to be unhappy with some element of your product or service, they might not want to pay you on time or at all, and they might give bad word of mouth and actually harm your brand. So why would you take them on as a client?

By completing this Personal Branding process I am confident that you can build a specific brand and market yourself effectively so that you can have some control over who you work with. It takes hard work and time to build your personal platform and attraction marketing campaign, but in the long term you will gain financial rewards and satisfaction in your work and life. Trust in the process and you will reap the benefits. There are no shortcuts, so persist and you will be successful.

To define your perfect client we will employ a common marketing technique that I have used many times when running large corporate campaigns. When marketing generic products that suit a large range of people, it is very challenging to create a marketing position to build an advertising campaign around. I distinctly remember trying to brief one of the largest marketing agencies in Australia about a million-dollar campaign and they were just not getting what I wanted. So we used the process I'm about to describe, to define what the product would mean for just one person – that is, the perfect client. The campaign we went on to devise was highly successful because although we aimed it at just one person, it still resonated with many others with a similar need.

The way I explain the process is with a bell curve. The peak of the bell curve is your perfect client, and on either side are clients that are not quite perfect but still a great fit for your product or service. The more you move yourself away from the centre of the bell curve, the less likely these clients are to want your product or service or be satisfied if they purchase it. If you aim for the perfect customer you will get a range of clients either side of them who fit your product or service and brand well. It is your choice how broad a catchment away from the perfect client you want to attract – it might be twenty or forty per cent of the total available clients, depending on how specific your product or service is and how far you need your reach to be to meet your goals.

Let's use an example to clarify how this works. Steve Jobs created Apple Ltd., one of the best companies in the world (and who created the product on which I type this book). Steve had a very specific Personal Brand; it was attractive to many people as his vision was inspirational, yet his products suited many people. Who is the perfect Apple client? I am sure there is an answer to this, yet their customer base has expanded rapidly to most of the world. However, not everyone is a fan of Apple because of their technology restrictions. Basically, you are either an Apple person or you are not – and this model works just fine for them. You can't please everyone in the world, so please the clients you want and don't worry about the rest.

To define your perfect client, close your eyes and think about the person you would most like to work with. How old are they, what gender are they, where do they live, what do they do, how wealthy are they, how educated are they? Then think about how they would work with you and react to your product or service; how you would contact and communicate with them; and how they would recommend you to their friends and colleagues.

Once you have a full mental image of this client, write all these details down. You will probably discover that your perfect client matches your values and working preferences. We like to spend time with people who are like us. So if you value your privacy, you might have a formal relationship with a client via email, and once you fulfil your service to them, there is limited contact. Alternatively, you might like socialising with clients and after the job you become friends and keep in touch on Facebook. Each to their own – there are no right or wrong clients, just those who suit you best.

Once you have defined your market and perfect client, it is time to network!

YOUR PERSONAL PITCH

I have a passion for pitching. It is so important to have a great answer when people ask you, 'So what do you do?' Most people give their title or a brief answer, thinking the other person isn't really interested. What a wasted opportunity! Of course the level of interest some will have in your Personal Business depends on who they are, where you meet them and what your business is. That said, you will never know if your business is of interest to them if you don't let them know what it is. More importantly, they might have a friend, family member or colleague that could be a perfect fit for your services, and you could miss an opportunity if you can't clearly and succinctly articulate your value to them.

There are many ways to pitch and my version is very simple, so you can remember it easily and use it just about anywhere. It has three parts: what is the problem, what is the solution and why are you best to solve it. It doesn't matter what order you deliver it or when you get to each section, just as long as you mention all three areas. So let's review an example to see how it works. Imagine you are at a function and someone asks you that golden question, 'What do you do?' You are standing with them so you have some knowledge about who they are and their situation. You can see their clothes, might know what they do and can make some judgement about what they are interested in. Your response should be tailored to them and the situation, and never, ever be rote learned. The more natural and from the heart it is, the better; it doesn't have to be perfect, just clear.

When people ask me that question, some of the answers I give include, '*You know how hard it is to keep up to date with all the social media programs and websites out there*' (the problem), '*well, I explain how to use these to make people look amazing online*' (the solution), at which time they normally are interested and want to know more, so I tell them more. '*I worked in corporate marketing for fifteen years creating amazing product brands, but I really love working with people so now I help people create businesses out of their brands'* (the why). I try to keep it conversational and fit in with their answers so it flows and feels natural. Practise it on your friends and you will be amazed at how many people ask you for your card and want you to contact them. If they are genuinely interested in your business you will not have to be pushy or ask for a meeting, they will ask you. This is the essence of a Personal Business – getting your perfect client to find you – and if you follow this process, you can have a business and life that you love. Good luck!

Conclusion

Congratulations on making the commitment to discovering more about yourself and what makes you unique, and taking steps to create a business you love.

As you worked through the three concepts of Understand, Build and Leverage in this book, you have considered what your brand looks like to an external audience, established the building blocks of your Personal Brand and learnt how to connect with the right audience.

I hope all of these tools will be very useful for your business, but I also hope that you have taken stock of the changes that have occurred in business and marketing mindsets in recent times. It is imperative that you have a new marketing mindset *before* constructing your Personal Brand. Not only will the old marketing mindset not work in new media, but you can destroy your brand and waste a lot of money. Learn how to add value to your customers, how to not sell to them, how to have two-way communication rather than one-way advertising, and you will do well. Basically, treat customers as you would like to be treated.

I thank you for taking the time to read this book. Regardless of how you found it, the important thing is that you have. Perhaps you think it was an accident. I personally don't believe in accidents – I think things happen for a reason – so if you have this book consider why it might be the perfect time for you to be reading it now. I've had some books gathering dust on my shelves for years and then have one day felt compelled to read them, strangely just at the perfect time to help me. If you have this book now it is possibly the perfect time to create your own Personal Business. Once you are done, please write a personal note in the front and pass the book on to someone you feel might need the knowledge or a boost. Books are a gift and knowledge is empowerment, so share the love!

I encourage you to join me on my social media and would love to hear your comments and experiences on constructing your Personal Brand. It is a new field and anything I can do to improve my methods is greatly appreciated. I hope to see you at one of my events, and if you ask me to sign your book I would be happy to. Until then, be brave and enjoy your new business and brand!

Next Steps

"I would love to hear your feedback and comments on the book so feel free to email me on andrew@andrewford.com.au, connect with me on LinkedIn au.linkedin.com/in/sirford or Facebook www.facebook.com/BeASocialStar and if you love Twitter feel free to add me @SirFord and #becomeasocialstar. I look forward to hearing from you!"

Social Star provides digital brand advice for small business and entrepreneurs. We love helping inspirational people shine online and if you need some additional support in getting your brand looking awesome try out web-based system for brand perfection at www.socialstar.com.au.

About the Author

Andrew Ford: 'The Brand Man'
www.andrewford.com.au

Marketing expert Andrew Ford, the founder of Social Star, has discovered the secret of the 'Personal Business'. With a fire for unleashing people's inner brand and developing business models to generate profit from an individual's passions, Andrew leverages ground-breaking digital and social media marketing techniques to create digital strategies for clients to attract maximum opportunities. Having established a strong name for himself in the field, Andrew blends traditional business techniques with now-necessary tools for entrepreneurs to achieve scale, quality, and influence in their niche.

Andrew's comprehensive business background and qualifications consist of a Bachelor of Business (Marketing) (RMIT 2003), a Graduate Certificate in Management (MBA Executive Program, University of Sydney 2005), and a Masters of

Entrepreneurship and Innovation (Swinburne University 2011). Continually on the cutting edge of his own education, Andrew has tested his marketing theories in forums such as the BCG Business Strategy Competition, which he won in 2005 against all Victorian MBA schools, and the Venture Cup Business Plan Competition (Swinburne University 2003), which he won in the Masters category. With experience working at Hewlett-Packard, Sensis (Telstra) and IBM, Andrew also has mentored dozens of junior staff to help them achieve their professional goals. Meeting and influencing high-profile public figures helped Andrew to realise just how many professionals require more understanding and control of their public brands or appearance, and need help with the skills to use the many amazing free tools at their disposal to generate success.

At Social Star, Andrew consults with clients to uncover their personal brand – both where it is today and where it can be tomorrow – and refine and define how that should be displayed in social media in order to attract their perfect target audience. Andrew mentors his clients to rapidly grow their business' audiences, resulting in larger potential client bases and higher revenue. Applying formulas that integrate over twenty years of Andrew's business experience and fifteen years of formal business education, Social Star specialises in building clarity and velocity for clients' brands using the 'Understand, Build and Leverage' methodology.

'Having a Personal Business enables people to have an authentic, congruent connection with their valued clients and partners, using their brand as the bridge,' says Andrew. 'I'm highly driven to work with the new breed of entrepreneurs and small business owners – people who have a passion for making the world a better place. Traditional business models are stepping aside as people follow their innermost dreams and my role is to see them operate within their values while creating wealth. Some people think you have to sacrifice what you to love to be successful in your business, yet it is actually the opposite. Follow your passion and success will come.'

Lecturing at Swinburne University from 2009 to 2011 on brand dynamics and digital marketing, presenting at numerous conferences, and consulting to hundreds of clients, Andrew has seen his philosophy work: that if you follow your unique path, based on your skills, experience, values and goals, you will automatically attract the opportunities you desire and achieve the success you deserve. Living his mantra, Andrew has created a successful business and attracts high-profile clients including musicians, athletes, authors, models, entrepreneurs, professionals and small business owners, helping them find their 'why' in their business and fulfilment in their lives.

Business for Andrew is more than work; it's personal. Running a personal business means that he is able to fulfil all of his values rather than separating his life from work. It supports his two boys while providing social opportunities, educational development, fitness opportunities, spiritual fulfilment and many valuable friendships. Social Star has now become the vehicle for Andrew to crystallise his mission in the world: to help people love what they do, supporting his 'why', that if more people loved what they did, the world would be a better place.

Published in 2014 in Australia by Andrew Ford

andrew@socialstar.com.au
www.socialstar.com.au

Text copyright © Andrew Ford 2014
Book Production: OpenBook Creative
Cover Design: Chantilly Creative
Cover Photo: Peter Marko
Editor: Brooke Clark

Australia Cataloguing-in-Publication entry

Author: Ford, Andrew
Title: Creating a Powerful Brand: It's not just business, it's personal

9781925144055 (paperback)
9781925144062 (ebook : epub)
9781925144079 (ebook : kindle)

Subjects: Small business - Australia - Management
          Branding (Marketing) - Management
          Marketing - Technological Innovations.

Dewey Number: 658.8

Disclaimer: Although the author and publisher have made every effort to ensure that the information in this book was correct at press time, the author and publisher do not assume and hereby disclaim any liability to any party for any loss, damage, or disruption caused by errors or omissions, whether such errors or omissions result from negligence, accident, or any other cause.

www.ingramcontent.com/pod-product-compliance
Lightning Source LLC
Chambersburg PA
CBHW071644210326
41597CB00017B/2103